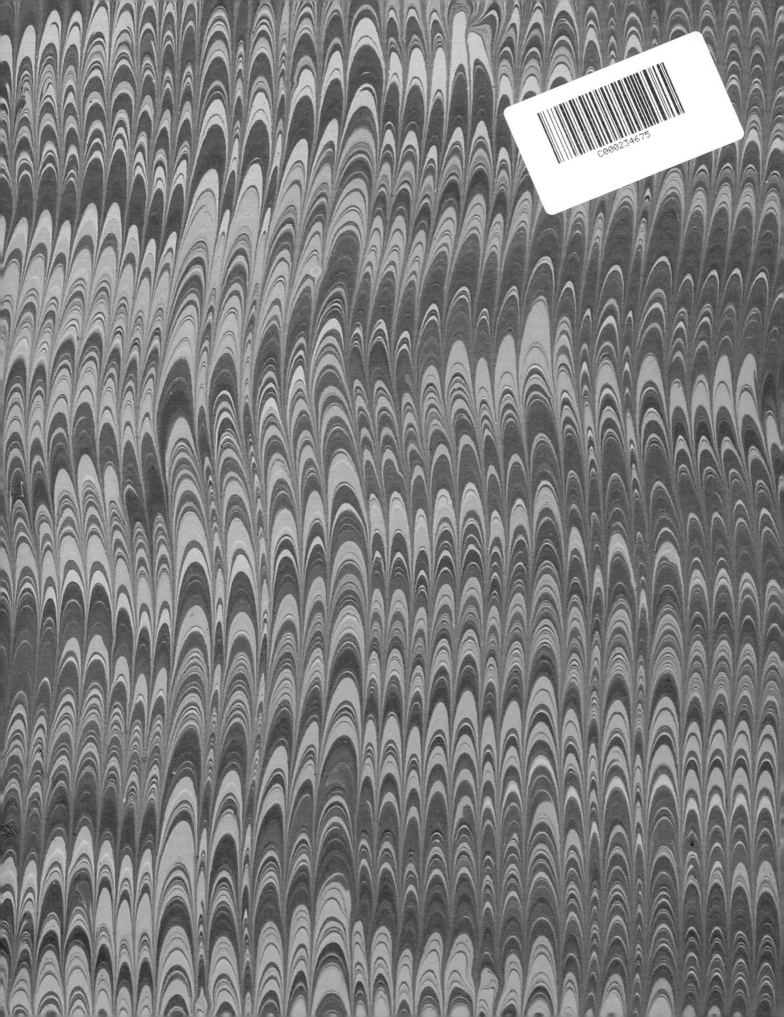

# Lord Byron's Best Friends
## from bulldogs to *Boatswain* and beyond

Including a complete facsimile of Elizabeth Pigot's illustrated poem of 1807
### *"The Wonderful History of Lord Byron & His Dog"*

## GEOFFREY BOND

The armorial achievement of the author

Published & produced by Nick McCann Associates Ltd 2013

Foreword by Loyd Grossman

# Foreword
## by Loyd Grossman

Two of London's most unusual public monuments face each other across the motorway that is Park Lane: Richard Westmacott's colossal Achilles, in tribute to the Duke of Wellington, and Richard Belt's statue of Lord Byron. With its rampant nudity, Achilles was said to have shocked the ladies who commissioned it in honour of England's hero. Belt's Byron is more subtly unsatisfactory, with the great poet looking like a dejected ex-member of a boy band in the introspective pose canonised by Raphael and Durer. What most distinguishes Belt's Byron though, is the vigour with which he modelled and the prominence which he gave to Byron's beloved Newfoundland dog, Boatswain. Indeed there is no finer sculptural portrait of a dog in London. And Boatswain does a fine job of mediating between us, the ordinary members of the public, and the stellar genius of the poet. As is often the case with portraits of the great – I am thinking for example of Titian's Charles V Standing With His Dog in the Prado – it is, ironically, the dog that humanizes the man.

*For my wife Dianora*

**Inner case:**

*Silhouette of Byron aged 18*
*& Boatswain's epitaph*


**Half title page:**

**The Byron Memorial Statue in Hyde Park (engraving)**
English School (20th century)

Richard Belt's (1851 – 1920) bronze of 1880 is situated
on a roundabout at the south end of Park Lane, London

The Illustrated London News Picture Library, London, UK / The Bridgeman Art Library


First published in the United Kingdom in 2013 by Nick McCann Associates Ltd
Design & Editorial by Nick Hugh McCann
Assisted by Sarah Davison

British Library Cataloguing-in-Publication Data
A catalogue record for this book is available from the British Library
ISBN 978-0-9516891-1-0

Printed and bound in China by 1010 Printing Ltd

For all enquiries and to order copies of this book please email:
consultancy@gbond.demon.co.uk

# Contents

Near this Spot
are deposited the Remains of one
who possessed Beauty without Vanity,
Strength without Insolence,
Courage without Ferosity,
and all the virtues of Man without his Vices.
This praise, which would be unmeaning Flattery
if inscribed over human Ashes,
is but a just tribute to the Memory of
BOATSWAIN, a DOG,
who was born in Newfoundland May 1803
and died at Newstead Nov.ʳ 18ᵗʰ 1808.

When some proud Son of Man returns to Earth,
Unknown to Glory but upheld by Birth,
The sculptor's art exausts the pomp of woe,
And storied urns record who rests below;
When all is done, upon the Tomb is seen
Not what he was, but what he should have been:
But the poor Dog, in life the firmest friend,
The first to welcome, foremost to defend,
Whose honest heart is still his Master's own,
Who labours, fights, lives, breathes for him alone,
Unhonour'd falls, unnotic'd all his worth,
Deny'd in heaven the Soul he held on earth:
While man, vain insect! hopes to be forgiven,
And claims himself a sole exclusive heaven.
Oh man! thou feeble tenant of an hour,
Debas'd by slavery, or corrupt by power,
Who knows thee well, must quit thee with disgust,
Degraded mass of animated dust!
Thy love is lust, thy friendship all a cheat,
Thy tongue hypocrisy, thy heart deceit!
By nature vile, ennobled but by name,
Each kindred brute might bid thee blush for shame.

The Author at
Boatswain's tomb,
Newstead Abbey, with
Newfoundlands:
Cruz (left) and Damian.

**Photograph by
Nigel Gibson**

# Introduction

My interest in Byron goes back to my youth, when I visited the printing press in my local museum at Newark-on-Trent, Nottinghamshire, used by S & J Ridge to print the poet's first verses, 'Fugitive Pieces' (1806) and 'Hours of Idleness' (1807).

I never expected that many years later, in 1990, I would become the owner of Burgage Manor in nearby Southwell – rented by the poet's mother Catherine Gordon during Byron's time at Harrow School and Trinity College Cambridge, between 1803 and 1808. My Byron collection has grown considerably over the years and features first editions, letters written from Burgage Manor, pictures and other Byron memorabilia.

While I am not sure I would have got on with Byron (some of his behaviour would not have been to my liking), I admire hugely his mind and the great influence that he had on the intellectual thought of the 19th century. His writing still has a powerful resonance today – his epic poem 'Don Juan' is one of the greatest pieces of satirical writing in the English language – and he was also a wonderful writer of letters. Thank goodness there were no computers and no emails in Byron's day so much of the archive has survived – no inbox to clear, no delete button to press! Byron and his contemporaries are a continuing source of interest and discovery – he must surely have spawned more English Literature PhD's than any other poet!

The Byron oeuvre is great, yet there is one subject which has never been specifically explored, namely his love of animals, and dogs in particular. In 2001, I wrote an article for the Newfoundland Journal on Byron and his famous dog, Boatswain,

and often discussed the subject with two old friends, Gerald Pendred and the Rt Hon Michael Foot PC, both now sadly deceased. I am indebted to them for their thoughts on the subject. Following this first foray into the world of Byron and his dogs, I was encouraged by friends to collect all the material I had on the subject – the result is this book.

The book has been put together by my friend, colleague, artist and fellow Byron enthusiast, Nick Hugh McCann, whom I first met when I bought his painting *Lord Byron's Last Journey* in 1989. Having once performed on stage as the dying Byron, alongside the Rt Hon Michael Foot and a huge Newfoundland dog, he is eminently qualified for the job! Nick has brought his creative flair and artist's eye to the project, sourcing many exciting and hitherto unpublished images. To my knowledge, the fascinating illustrated poem, 'The Wonderful History of Lord Byron and his Dog' (1807), by the young Byron's Southwell neighbour Elizabeth Pigot, has never previously been reproduced in its entirety in colour.

Byron has given me a great deal of interest and fun over the years, working with colleagues at international conferences, running Byron societies, writing and making films. He has brought me so many friends around the world, a huge dividend from the study of this amazing man and his times.

Geoffrey Bond
Burgage Manor, Southwell
2013

## Living with a Legend

Southwell in Nottinghamshire was, in Byron's day, a sleepy Austen-esque town which the burgeoning poet found somewhat dull and unexciting. Today, Byron may still recognise much of his Southwell; little has changed. Burgage Manor was where Byron wrote much of his early poetry and the house has many reminders of his life and times.

**Above:** *Southwell Minster in Byron's day*
Oil on canvas
Artist unknown
Private Collection

**Below:** *Bust of Byron*
Lorenzo Bartolini, 1822
*'It resembles a superannuated Jesuit - I cannot be long for this world - for it overlooks 70.'*

*Burgage Manor House as it was when Ld Byron lived there & first printed his poems in 1806*

**Above:**

Byron's neighbour, Elizabeth Pigot, has left us a unique picture of the youthful Lord's love of dogs in her illustrated poem, *"The Wonderful History of Lord Byron & His Dog"* – featured later in the book. Her drawing gives us an equally unique record of how his home looked at the time; *'Burgage Manor House as it was when Ld Byron lived here & first printed his poems in 1806.'* The window (middle row right), was Byron's bedroom.

**Right:**
***Burgage Manor today***

Photographs:
Nick Hugh McCann

# The Life of Lord Byron

The poet Byron was George Gordon Byron, 6th Baron Byron of Rochdale. Born 22nd January 1788 in London, he succeeded to the title in 1798 and died in his 36th year on 19th April, 1824, in the town of Missolonghi in Western Greece.

He was the cause of controversy, a charismatic figure, a colossus on the European stage and one of England's first great pan-Europeans. Byron's life was so full of excitement, so varied and so full of contradictions that he has been a continuing source of interest to generations. It could be said that Byron gave rise to the first 'Fan Club'. He was famous in his day, and unlike some of his contemporaries – Shelley, Keats and Coleridge – was an enormous financial and literary success during his lifetime. In a letter which he wrote in September 1813 to Annabella Milbanke, the woman who was to become his wife, he wrote, 'The great object of life is sensation – to feel that we exist, even though in pain. It is this "craving void" which drives us to gaming – to battle – to travel – to intemperate but keenly felt pursuits of every description, whose principal attraction is the agitation inseparable from their accomplishment.'

Byron's father 'Mad Jack Byron' died soon after Byron's birth, so the boy was brought up in a one-parent family. He had a congenital disability which made him lame in his right leg, giving him a pronounced limp. His ancestors paved the way for his extraordinary personality: his father was a womaniser and died of drink; several of his relatives were involved in outrageous incidents, and his mother – a short dumpy Aberdonian Scot – was of a temperamental disposition.

**A woman alone...**
'That Boy will be the death of me, & drive me mad.
I never will consent to his going abroad.'

***Catherine Gordon Byron***
Oil on canvas
T. Stewardson

John Murray Collection

**'That Beautiful Pale Face is My Fate'**
So said the unstable Caroline Lamb when she first met the
poet later in life. This likeness was one of Byron's favourites,
but the beatific countenance belied a tempestuous inner life.

***Lord Byron aged 27***
Watercolour on ivory miniature - James Holmes

Private Collection

**Put on a pedestal**
Even today Byron is revered in
Greece as a national hero.
Over the spot where his lungs
are buried in the town of
Missolonghi, stands this statue
of 'Lordos Vironos'.

***Byron's Monument at
Missolonghi, Greece***
Nicolas Himona, 1923

Nottingham City Museums and Galleries,
Newstead Abbey

### Pale Rider

'Born half a Scot and bred a whole one' he once wrote; Byron's early years in Scotland had a profound impact on his self-image. The Gordon plaid he wore as a child would reappear regularly as part of his flamboyant dress: 'My heart warms to the tartan.'

*A recreation of young Byron in the Highlands, with his first love, Mary Duff.*

*Visions of Byron*
© Nick Hugh McCann

For the first ten years of his life (1788-1798) Byron lived in ordinary circumstances in Aberdeen with his widowed mother, and developed a Scottish lilt to his speech which, while it diminished, remained with him for the rest of his life. Not being able to run as fast as ordinary boys, Byron found alternative ways in which he could keep up – he was good at boxing, pistol shooting and swimming. His disability did not seem to affect his success with the ladies in later life. At the time when he was attending fashionable London balls, between 1811 and 1815, the waltz was scandalising society and, although Byron could not dance, women flocked around him.

Byron admires actresses at one of London's fashionable theatres.

### Lobby Loungers

*(taken from the Saloon of the Drury Lane Theatre)*
Hand-coloured engraving by George Cruikshank

Byron's image and lifestyle made great material for the satirists of the time.

Private Collection

LOBBY Loungers. (taken from the Saloon of Drury Lane Theatre)

'The Brig of Don near the "auld toun" of Aberdeen with its one arch, and its black deep salmon stream below, is my memory as yesterday.'

*View of The Brig of Balgownie, Old Aberdeen*
Oil on canvas
Artist unknown,
*c.* 1830-40

© Aberdeen Art Gallery
& Museums Collections

Byron grew up to be a rather overweight, bashful boy, 5ft 8$\frac{1}{2}$in and 14st – later to slim down to around 11st for most of his life. Not only did slimming enhance his good looks, it also kept the weight off his bad leg and allowed him to walk more easily. Sir Walter Scott described Byron's countenance as like an alabaster vase lit from within. He had a pale, mysterious, brooding countenance with dark brown curly hair, blue-grey eyes, a noble forehead, a good strong jaw-line, a head set on a muscular neck and shoulders tapering down to slim hips; the build of an athlete.

Byron also had a mercurial temperament. One day he would greet a friend heartily, and the next regard him with disdain. There is evidence to show he suffered from anorexia nervosa and bulimia, and was possibly also a manic depressive. He did have great mood swings. Temperamental genius often goes hand in hand with such conditions. He was often extremely kind to those in less fortunate circumstances.

In 1794, as a schoolboy in Aberdeen, a monumental event changed his life forever. His cousin was killed at the Siege of Calvi in Corsica, precipitating Byron into line to become the 6th Baron Byron of Rochdale when the 5th Lord, his great-uncle died. This came to pass four years later, in 1798, when the ten-year-old Byron and his mother travelled down from Aberdeen to see the Newstead Abbey estate in Nottinghamshire. Byron and his mother lived at various lodgings in Nottingham before she rented Burgage Manor in Southwell while Byron was at Harrow School and Trinity College, Cambridge between 1803 and 1808.

Byron's sexual awakening was early. There is evidence to show that he was abused by his nurse May Gray as a small boy. At the age of 15 or 16, he fell desperately in love with Mary Chaworth of Annesley, near to Newstead Abbey and this experience led him to write in 1806 his first juvenile book of verse, printed under the title 'Fugitive Pieces'. Byron's rejection by Mary Chaworth affected him deeply. When, unobserved in the grounds of Annesley Hall, he overheard Mary's maid ask her whether she would marry the young Lord Byron, she replied, 'me! marry that lame brat, never!' Byron carried this emotional scar with him throughout his life.

Although living in Southwell, Byron did visit Newstead Abbey from time to time. There was a tenant, Lord Grey de Ruthyn, and something happened – possibly Grey tried to interfere with the young Byron. Whatever the truth, he never returned while Grey was in occupation.

On going to Cambridge University, Byron did very little work, indulging himself instead in wine, women and song and enjoying some – probably platonic – relationships with a number of younger men. He formed a particular friendship with John Cam Hobhouse, later in life to become Lord Broughton, which he was to maintain for the rest of his life and with whom he went on his first trip abroad to Greece and Albania.

**Opposite:**
*Come back to my place*

Byron's image was enhanced by the mansion he had back in the provinces; part being the crumbling romantic monastery, Newstead Abbey in Nottinghamshire.

*Newstead Abbey, Nottinghamshire*
Oil on canvas
Henry Bright

Nottingham City Museums and Galleries

**Left:**
*Bee-littled*

Mary Chaworth left the gawky young Byron devastated by her waspish comments. When famous, he enjoyed rejecting her advances for a re-match.

*Miniature of Mary Chaworth*

*It's academic*
Byron may have dressed the part but didn't lift a finger at Cambridge, save to feed his tame bear. He did however receive his MA!

**Opposite:**
*The young pretender*

Byron's epic poem *Childe Harold* might have been set in Scotland, or never written at all, if Byron had ventured to the Hebrides, his initial plan. This swashbuckling image shows the extravagant young Lord with his page, Robert Rushton.

***George Gordon, 6th Lord Byron***
Oil on canvas
George Sanders, 1809
© HM The Queen

**Below:**
*The first tourist*

What a cast & crew. With camels and exhausted Albanian guards as part of his retinue, the passionate poet reclines beside a conveniently discarded doric remnant.

***Lord Byron's 'Dream'***
Oil on canvas
Sir Charles Lock Eastlake
(1793 – 1865)
© Tate, London 2013

When Byron first went abroad in 1809, Napoleon was still fighting wars through Europe, so Byron went from Falmouth to Lisbon in Portugal, across southern Spain through Seville to Cadiz, and from there to Gibraltar, along the southern Mediterranean and into Western Greece.

Here his free spirit soared as, untrammelled by the oppressive manners of Regency society, he was able to indulge himself in a wide range of pursuits not available to him in London. Byron was captivated by the Albanians and their warlike personalities and visited the notorious ruler Ali Pasha at his fortress in Tepellene. Looking at Byron's soft white hands, Ali asked him to meet with him after supper – Byron declined the offer.

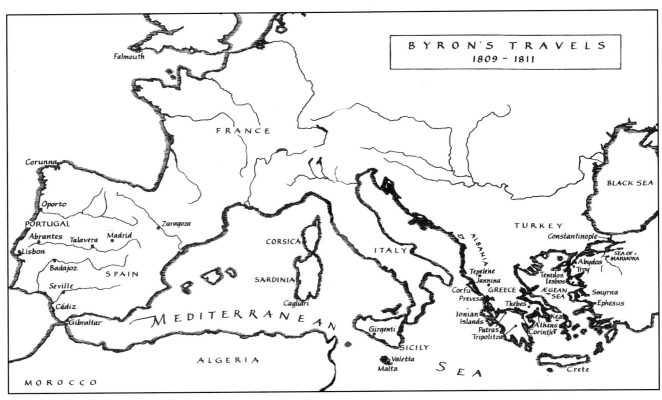

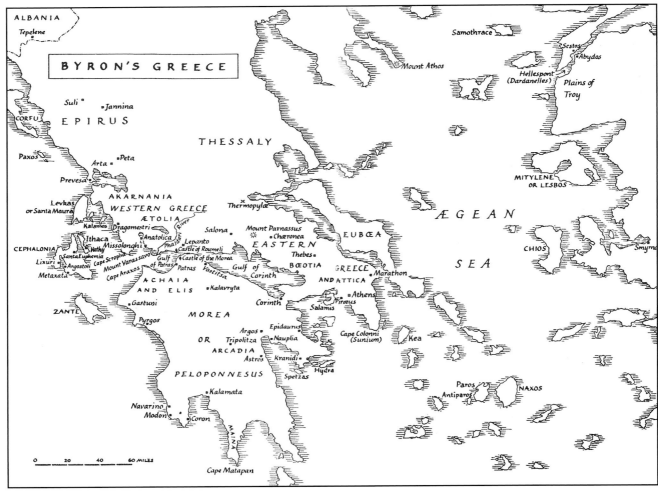

### Red sails in the sunset

Byron's first sight of the Continent – the entrance to the Tagus at Lisbon, Portugal, and the picturesque castle of Belém.

***The Tower of Belém, Lisbon, Portugal***
Oil on canvas
Frank Dillon, *c.* 1850

Guildhall Art Gallery,
City of London Corporation

### Hero worship

The Battle of Trafalgar in 1805 was a pivotal moment in the Napoleonic Wars (1803 – 1815). When Byron arrived in Portugal and Spain in 1809, he always made sure he wore a scarlet British regimental uniform, to leave the residents in no doubt which side he was on.

***The 'Victory' Towed into Gibralter***
Oil on panel
Clarkson Frederick Stansfield, 1854

Guildhall Art Gallery,
City of London Corporation

### Romance

The poet's stay in Valetta, Malta, turned out to be a very romantic affair; he fell violently in love with Mrs Constance Spencer Smith, someone else's wife...

***The 'Princess Charlotte'
in Malta Harbour***
Oil on canvas
Johann Schranz, *c.* 1828

Government Art Collection

### Graffiti Artist

A must-see on today's culture tour of Greece, in Byron's day Cape Sunium was a much more remote place. Wild dogs are part of Turner's suitably Byronic vision of the place which so inspired the poet. Despite the reverence, Byron thought it appropriate to carve his name in one of the pillars – still to be seen today...

**The Temple of Poseidon at Sunium (Cape Colonna)**
Pencil, watercolour and gouache on paper
Joseph Mallord William Turner
(1793 – 1851), *c.* 1834

© Tate, London 2013

*The isles of Greece, the isles of Greece!*
*Where burning Sappho loved and sung,*
*Where grew the arts of war and peace,*
*Where Delos rose, and Phoebus sprung!*
*Eternal summer gilds them yet,*
*But all, except their sun, is set...*

*The mountains look on Marathon –*
*And Marathon looks on the sea;*
*And musing there an hour alone,*
*I dreamed that Greece might still be free;*
*For standing on the Persians' grave,*
*I could not deem myself a slave.*

*A king sat on the rocky brow*
*Which looks o'er sea-born Salamis;*
*And ships, by thousands, lay below,*
*And men in nations – all were his!*
*He counted them at break of day –*
*And when the sun set, where were they?*

*Place me on Sunium's marbled steep,*
*Where nothing, save the waves and I,*
*May hear our mutual murmurs sweep;*
*There, swanlike, let me sing and die:*
*A land of slaves shall ne'er be mine –*
*Dash down yon cup of Samian wine!*

From Don Juan Canto III

*Lord Byron and Sir Walter Scott at No. 50 Albemarle Street, 1815*

Byron returned to England in 1811 having written two Cantos of his first major poem, 'Childe Harold's Pilgrimage'. Published in March 1812, it made him famous overnight. Byron continued to write and was an immediate best seller, some of his new works selling as many as 10,000 copies on the day of publication. He accumulated through his publisher, John Murray, considerable royalties which he disdained to take, even though at times he was being pursued by his creditors for unpaid debts. These new works included 'The Giaour' and 'The Bride of Abydos' in 1813, 'The Corsair' and 'Lara' in 1814, and 'The Siege of Corinth' and 'Parisina' in 1816.

Here was a handsome mysterious outsider with a title who had captured the hearts and minds of not only the women of his time in England, but many of the men as well. However, his peers kept their distance and he had little support when trying to enter the House of Lords to make his maiden speech in February 1812. In fact he made three speeches: in defence of the framework knitters of Nottinghamshire; for Catholic emancipation, and for Parliamentary reform. Byron was a Whig and disliked the Tory establishment and the Monarchy. While he was not a democrat in today's terms, he was far in advance of his peers in his political thinking about fairness in society.

Byron hated hypocrisy and sanctimony and resented one nation oppressing another. It was this philosophy which led him, in 1824 – the final year of his life – to help the Greeks rid themselves of the Ottoman Turks.

### 'Singing in the rain'

'Weather Wise – One day on a voyage to Athens, a dark cloud appeared to windward, his Lordship regarded it steadily for some time, until at length feeling a few drops of rain fall, he called to Fletcher to bring his cloak, so certain he was of an approaching shower'.

**Anecdotes of Byron -**
**or a touch of the marvellous**

Charles Williams
1813

*Competing to be the Poet Laureate*

The political satirists of the Regency era made our tabloid media and television commentators look very tame indeed. The absent Byron is represented by his publisher, John Murray, in black, carrying Byron's works.

In this classically-themed panorama, 'Rival Candidates for the Vacantbays', the Regent is seen cavorting on a barrel of wine (with the inscription '£100 per annum' on its side).

*Rival Candidates for the Vacantbays*
London Publish'd Oct 1st 1813 by N. Jones, 5 Newman Street
Coloured engraving

Private Collection

*The West End in 1737*

A colourful and chaotic Covent Garden, London, as it would have looked just prior to Byron's day: dogs, open-air prize-fighting, market traders mixing it with the hoi polloi, and the aristocracy out to see how the other half lived.

*Covent Garden Market and St Paul's Church, London*
Balthasar Nebot
*c.* 1737

Guildhall Art Gallery,
City of London Corporation

**'The Princess of Paralellograms'**
...is what Byron called his methodical and mathematical bride. Their daughter Ada (Byron's only legitimate child) became Charles Babbage's assistant in creating his 'Difference Engine', the forebear of all our computers today. The computer language *Ada*, created on behalf of the United States Department of Defense, was named after her.

***Lady Byron (Annabella Milbanke)***
Coloured engraving

**Lower left:**
*Love & Marriage*

Byron & Annabella's marriage was a sham, and it ended badly for all concerned.

***Wedding certificate of 1815 at Seaham, County Durham***

**Below:**
*Bitter Harvest*

Lady Byron endeavoured to poison her daughter's mind against Byron, but Ada remained stoic to her father's memory. When she died at 36 – the same age as the poet – she was buried next to him in Hucknall church, at her request.

***Lady Byron in old age***
Daguerreotype

In terms of his relationships with women, Byron had a number of great loves in his life, one of whom was undoubtedly his half-sister Augusta Leigh, whom he got to know in his late teens. Although she was a half-blood relative, their suspected incestuous relationship scandalised society.

On 2nd January 1815 Byron married Annabella Milbanke, by whom he had a daughter, Ada. Like her mother, Ada (who married the 1st Lord Lovelace) was a good mathematician and went on to become famous in her own right, helping Charles Babbage develop the Analytical Engine – a first form of computer – before emulating her father and paternal grandfather and dying at the age of 36. Byron had an illegitimate child by Clare Clairmont – a daughter called Allegra who died at the age of five years – and there is argument to say that he also had a daughter called Medora by his half-sister, Augusta Leigh.

### Stormy Weather

In 1816, when Byron left England, a hounded man, his loyal friend Hobhouse recalled seeing him off from Dover: '*I ran to the end of the wooden pier – and as the vessel toss'd by as through a rough sea & contrary wind saw him again – the dear fellow pulled off his cap & wav'd it to me.*' Sixteen hellish hours later the ship arrived in Ostend. Byron recalled, '*stomached the sea pretty well till a damned "Merchant of Bruges" capsized his breakfast close by me, and made me sick by contagion.*'

### Ostend Packet - in a Squall
George Cruikshank; George Humphrey

OSTEND Packet - in a SQUALL

# FARE THEE WELL.

FARE thee well! and if for ever—
  Still for ever, fare *thee well*.—
Even though unforgiving, never
  'Gainst thee shall my heart rebel.
Would that breast were bared before thee
  Where thy head so oft hath lain,
While that placid sleep came o'er thee
  Which thou ne'er canst know again:
Would that breast by thee glanc'd over,
  Every inmost thought could show!
Then, thou would'st at last discover
  'Twas not well to spurn it so—
Though the world for this commend thee—
  Though it smile upon the blow,
Even its praises must offend thee,
  Founded on another's woe—
Though my many faults defac'd me;
  Could no other arm be found
Then the one which once embraced me
  To inflict a cureless wound?
Yet—oh, yet—thyself deceive not—
  Love may sink by low decay,
But by sudden wrench, believe not,
  Hearts can thus be torn away;
Still thine own its life retaineth—
  Still must mine—though bleeding—beat,
And the undying thought which paineth
  Is—that we no more may meet.—
These are words of deeper sorrow
  Than the wail above the dead,

Both shall live—but every morrow
  Wake us from a widowed bed.—
And when thou would'st solace gather—
  When our child's first accents flow—
Wilt thou teach her to say "Father!"
  Though his care she must forego?
When her little hands shall press thee—
  When her lip to thine is press'd—
Think of him whose prayer shall bless thee—
  Think of him thy love had bless'd,
Should her lineaments resemble
  Those thou never more may'st see—
Then thy heart will softly tremble
  With a pulse yet true to me.
All my faults—perchance thou knowest—
  All my madness—none can know;
All my hopes—where'er thou goest—
  Wither—yet with *thee* they go—
Every feeling hath been shaken,
  Pride—which not a world could bow—
Bows to thee—by thee forsaken
  Ev'n my soul forsakes me now.
But 'tis done—all words are idle—
  Words from me are vainer still;
But the thoughts we cannot bridle
  Force their way without the will.
Fare thee well!—thus disunited—
  Torn from every nearer tie—
Seared in heart—and lone—and blighted—
  More than this I scarce can die.

PUBLISHED BY J. JOHNSTON, CHEAPSIDE.

*Becoming a European*

Despite collosal debts, Byron's exile south to Switzerland was facilitated by his commissioning in London – prior to his hasty exit – of a copy of the Emperor Bonaparte's huge Imperial coach. Byron's coach broke down outside Brussels and they had to enter the city for repairs.

*Hôtel de Ville,*
*Brussels, Belgium*
Oil on canvas
François Stroobant, 1870

Guildhall Art Gallery,
City of London Corporation

**Opposite:**
*Hoisted by his own petard*

Byron's ditty, 'Fare Thee Well', became excellent ammunition for this sketch writer and satirist. The paunchy poet is seen abandoning his wife and child, accompanied by actresses (including Mrs Mardyn of the Drury Lane Theatre), copious bottles of wine ('Old Hock') and his much-derided skull cup to drink them from. The jolly tars on the ship provide further intellectual comment: 'I say Jack I hopes he's got enough on 'em aboard!' 'Yes & may I never take another bit of Shag if they arn't fine vessels.'

*Fare thee well*
Hand-coloured engraving
George Cruikshank
Pub. John Johnston, April 1816

Why he married Annabella Milbanke one will never know; she was quite unsuited to him. The marriage did not last very long – even on his honeymoon Byron described it as his 'treacle moon'. By mid-January 1816 Annabella had left him, citing his intolerable behaviour towards her, and she devoted her life to doing all she could to destroy his reputation, never letting him see Ada and denigrating him at every opportunity. Ostracised by London society because of his behaviour, Byron left England in April 1816, never to return.

He travelled to Switzerland where, in the famous wet summer of 1816, he lived close to Clare Clairmont (with whom he had a daughter, Allegra), Percy Shelley, Mary Shelley and his physician Dr John Polidori. The stories they produced between them became the subject of many 20th-century plays and films, including 'Frankenstein' and 'The Vampyre'.

Byron then moved to Italy, where he had tempestuous affairs with countless different women – just as in London he had had relationships with Lady Caroline Lamb, the Countess of Oxford and others. His most debauched time was in Venice, from where he wrote to his publisher John Murray in London, saying he'd had upward of 200 women that year. (Byron often exaggerated in his letters to Murray knowing they would be read by many other friends!)

On an excursion to Mont Blanc in August 1816, Byron recalled: 'In the very eyes of Mont Blanc' he had heard an Englishwoman exclaim to her party, '"Did you ever see anything more *rural*?" - as if it was Highgate, or Hampstead, or Brompton, or Hayes, – "*Rural!*" quotha! – Rocks, pines, torrents, Glaciers, Clouds, and Summits of eternal snow far above them – "*Rural!*"'

**Mont Blanc, Glacier des Bossons, Chamonix**
Oil on canvas
John Webber, 1788
(the year of Byron's birth)

Government Art Collection

***Dog days***

The satiated Venetian visitor slumps over his writing desk, with loyal dog in attendance.

**Byron's Room in Palazzo Mocenigo, Venice**
Watercolour on paper
English School, 19th century

Private Collection / The Stapleton Collection / The Bridgeman Art Library

Opposite:
**Dual Destination**

Byron's time in Venice was divided between summer on the mainland at La Mira, and winter at his residence on the Grand Canal, Palazzo Mocenigo.

**In the Gulf of Venice, Italy**
Oil on canvas
Clarkson Frederick Stanfield

Guildhall Art Gallery,
City of London Corporation

In January 1818 he met Countess Teresa Guiccioli – his last great passion. She lived in Ravenna with her husband Count Guiccioli who was content to let Byron be his wife's cavalier servante. In time, Teresa separated from her husband and lived with Byron until he left for Greece in late 1823.

One of Byron's most productive times was when he was living in Venice. He would typically rise towards midday, have a meal, go riding and swimming, then return to make love. Sometimes he made love before he went swimming as well as after! He would indulge in gossip with his vast household – which was also full of all kinds of pets, a virtual menagerie – and after carousing late into the evening he settled down to write until the early hours of the morning, accompanied by a steady supply of gin and water. He called his poetry the lava of his imagination.

*The horseman*

Lord Byron after his daily
ride at Pisa, 1822

It was during his debauched time in Venice that Byron wrote much of his satirical poem, 'Don Juan', thought by many to be his greatest work. He also produced other poems and plays, as well as writing copious letters home and giving thought to where he might go next. At one stage he considered going to South America, having been inspired by Simon Bolivar and others. Instead, Byron stayed in Italy and during the period from 1819 to 1823 he tried to help the Italians get rid of their Austrian masters. Ever supportive of the underdog, he was active in secret societies run by the Carbonari until he himself came under suspicion.

### Wish You Were Here

During his time in Italy, Byron ventured to many parts of the country to do some selective sightseeing. Florence (top) saw him visiting galleries, returning 'drunk with beauty', and en route across the Appenines, he was disappointed by his Swiss shepherd dog Mutz's timorous nature when he was routed by a pig. In Rome (above) he witnessed a hanging, and was immortalised in marble in a bust by Thorwaldsen. Genoa (right) was his last residence and the place where he commissioned another Byronic icon, the much-lampooned Homeric helmet he had made in preparation for his Greek Campaign.

**Top: The Ponte Vecchio, Florence**
Oil on canvas - Francesco Raffaello Santoro, 1888

**Above left: Coliseum, Rome**
Oil on canvas - Charles Lock Eastlake

**Above right: Street in Genoa, Italy**
Oil on canvas - James Holland

All images this page: Brighton and Hove Museums and Art Galleries

**Who pays the Ferryman**

Byron is seen being rowed out into the mephitic swamp, that lay beside early 19th century Missolonghi.

**Household cavalry**

Byron (centre, in the red jacket) riding his grey horse Mameluke, accompanied by his band of enthusiastic but chaotic Suliote soldiers outside the walls of the town.

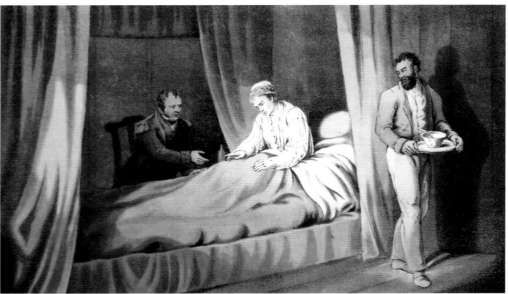

**White as a sheet**

The garrison Firemaster, William Parry, receives instructions from a dying Byron; his head bandaged from the copious application of leeches. Byron's loyal and fearsome Venetian gondolier, Tita Falcieri, removes soup from the scene.

Engravings by Robert Seymor from sketches by William Parry (1824)

Private Collection

*Real Estate*

Although Byron waxed lyrical about Newstead in his early poems, unusually he inherited the freehold and couldn't wait to sell it, and when the Greeks needed funds, it provided the necessary means.

***East View of Newstead Abbey, Nottinghamshire, and the Great Garden***
Oil on canvas
Richard Byron, 1758

Newstead Abbey,
Nottingham City Museums and Galleries

Byron was approached by the London Committee of the Philhellenes in the early 1820s because of his experience of Greece in 1809-1811. In 1817 Byron had sold Newstead Abbey, his ancestral home in Nottinghamshire, for nearly £98,000, severing his last links with England. He thus had considerable capital with which to build a boat, have it loaded with armaments, gold and provisions, and journey to Greece in July 1823.

Byron eventually arrived in Missolonghi in Western Greece, then a damp, marshy, malaria-ridden town. In late 1823 – some months after striking his head on the branch of a tree – he suffered a number of fits. He became ill and, on 19th April 1824, died at the age of 36. Modern medical views confirm Byron's death was severely hastened by the desanguination he underwent at the hands of his doctors.

*A soldier's death*

At Byron's hastily-arranged funeral in Missolonghi, a rough wooden box was used for a makeshift coffin and his Greek helmet was placed on top. His body was then shipped back to England in a barrel of spirits. The helmet is now on display at Newstead Abbey.

***Visions of Byron***
© Nick Hugh McCann

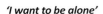

**'I want to be alone'**

Sensing things were looking
very bleak on all fronts,
Byron, despite his increasingly
frail health, would ride out
into the rain-sodden marshes,
accompanied by his faithful
Newfoundland, Lyon.
On one  of these rides he
caught a chill which hastened
the inevitable end.

The real cause of his demise
is still a matter of conjecture,
but it is thought that
desanguination by his doctors
made his death certain.

**Lord Byron's Last Journey**
Watercolour &
bodycolour on paper
Nick Hugh McCann, 1988

© Nick Hugh McCann
Private Collection

Byron did his best to organise the Greeks, but his Albanian or Suliote troops constantly squabbled and wasted his money. Byron died before fighting proper got underway and it was not until the Battle of Navarino in October 1827 that Greece won the War of Independence and her freedom. However, the fact that, as a wealthy and famous aristocrat, Lord Byron supported the Greek cause, has ensured his immortality and statues to his memory have been raised across the country. It is said that the whole of Europe mourned Byron's death and in Greece, he is a hero to this day.

Byron inspired generations of freedom fighters and was as famous in his time as Napoleon, Wellington and Nelson. His intellectual thought pervaded through the 19th century, directly influencing artists such as Turner and Delacroix and composers such as Berlioz, Schumann and Mendelssohn. The great German philosopher, Goethe, thought very highly of him.

Byron was a restless soul and never seemed to come to terms with himself or his fellow men and women, and certainly not the country of his birth. He was the quintessential outsider. In many ways he was ahead of his time, a modern man, and his writings even presaged the nuclear holocaust in his poem 'Darkness'.

Byron wrote of Freedom – 'thy banner torn but flying, Streams like the thunder-storm against the wind.' One's vision of Byron is standing heroically on a mountain promontory, wishing that nation would not oppress nation and using his enormous satirical skills in his verse to parody and pinprick the balloons of the pompous. He was one of the best verbal cartoonists there has ever been. But there was a dark side to Byron, too. He constantly sought the love and affection which had been denied him as a boy and his relationships with lovers, both men and women, were a reflection of this longing. Perhaps Byron's half-sister Augusta was really the only person who fully understood him and with whom he was completely at ease.

Whether one likes Byron's poetry or not, he was one of the greatest minds of his generation and for many scholars his work is second only to Shakespeare. He remains the subject of eternal fascination, with a huge following all over the world – a tribute to his multi-faceted personality and his status as one of the most intriguing men in history.

Byron may have found relationships with humans difficult but never with animals, which he loved (see Chapter 1, where his epitaph to his beloved dog Boatswain, is described). Like the poet Alexander Pope before him, Byron entered into the classical debate about the place of animals and whether or not they possess souls. Christine Kenyon-Jones in her book 'Kindred Brutes – Animals In Romantic-Period Writing' (2001) writes: 'A key part of the classical debate about the status of animals was the question of whether or not they possessed souls. Animists such as Pythagoras believed they did. Pope, the owner of at least two Great Danes, anthropomorphised his pet animals in verse but stays just short of stating his own belief in the immortality of animal souls. Byron shared Pope's views and had a great love of animals and dogs in particular.'

**Opposite:**
*Wearing the tartan*

Byron was fond of wearing tartan in Italy and on his rides in the Greek winter at Missolonghi. He would wrap himself in yards of plaid fabric he had brought especially for the campaign, and is portrayed here wearing the Gordon tartan.

Oil on canvas
Giralomo Prepiani, 1822

Private Collection

**Opposite:**
*Fine and Dandie*

Celtic novelist and poet;
*'Scott was perhaps the most
devoted dog lover that ever
was.'* - New York Times.

*Sir Walter Scott, 1771 - 1832,
Novelist and poet*
Oil on canvas
Sir William Adam

© The National Galleries of Scotland

Among Byron's good friends was Sir Walter Scott, who like Byron had a disability – he contracted polio as a boy and had a pronounced limp for the rest of his life. Scott and Byron first met in London in 1815 in John Murray's rooms in Albemarle Street. Scott loved Byron's poetry and Byron loved Scott's Waverley novels. Both had a huge compassion for animals and Scott had many in his household; dogs and cats, as well as a hen and a donkey which followed him around.

The world-famous Scott monument in Princes Street, Edinburgh, features a sculpture by Sir John Steell of Scott and his dog Maida, which he describes as a very large wolf-greyhound. At the other end of the country – situated on an island at the southern end of Park Lane where the constant traffic rushing around it makes it almost impossible to reach – is a statue of Byron and his beloved Boatswain by the sculptor Richard Belt.

Scott also owned Hamlet, a black greyhound, and as a child kept a dog called Snap, said to have been part bulldog. As Byron tried to save Boatswain's life, nursing him when he had rabies, so Scott with one of his dogs called Camp, saved its life by force-feeding it with milk in a teaspoon. Scott replaced Camp with a terrier which he described as 'the old shaggy Celtic breed'. Scott's love of terriers led to one of the most famous breeds, originally used to find foxes that had gone to earth, taking its name from one of his fictional creations – 'Dandie Dinmont', a farming character in his novel, 'Guy Mannering'.

NOTTINGHAM MARKET PLACE.
DEDICATED TO THE WORSHIPFULL THE MAYOR AND CORPORATION
BY THEIR MOST OBEDIENT SERVANT J.ROBERTSON THEATRE 1806.

### Man of The People

Byron would have known Nottingham Market Place — today termed 'Slab Square' — very well as a young boy fresh from Scotland. He lived on nearby St James Street when the picture above was drawn by J. Robertson and titled **Theatre 1806**. In the foreground is a Punch & Judy show and dressed-up performing dogs; in the background, various named shops and the local militia on a drill.

On a baking hot day in July 1824 Byron came back to his childhood Nottinghamshire home. His funeral procession left the yard of the Blackamore's Head Inn (just behind the large building centre right, now the Council House), and wended its way through the square and up the Mansfield Road to Hucknall, some miles north. On the day the scene must have resembled a modern celebrity or royal funeral, with literally thousands gathered at every corner trying to gain a glimpse of the vast cortege with six black horses bedecked with plumes, pulling a carriage with the draped ornate coffin decorated with his sword; the ordinary people of Nottingham thought of Byron as *theirs*. They had not forgotten his maiden speech in the House of Lords, championing the Nottinghamshire *Frame Breakers* and arguing for justice for the working man and woman.

### Tomb Raiders

When Byron's favourite dog Boatswain's extravagant tomb at Newstead Abbey was opened up for repairs in the late 1980s, it was discovered the dog's stone sarcophagus was broken and the coffin missing.

In 1938, permission was granted to inspect Byron's family vault in Hucknall church. Tantalisingly, although the coffin was photographed, the body was not. Byron's coffin is on the left, and his daughter Ada's, with the more intact coronet, lies to the right. Viewing the body, those present observed it was 'in an excellent state of preservation'.

***Pet cemetery***

Boatswain's tomb framed
by the West Front of
a wintry Newstead Abbey.

Photograph:
Nick Hugh McCann

Just as Byron throughout his life enjoyed the companionship of his dogs, so Scott said, 'The companionship of a dog seemed almost as necessary as a hat or a stick. A man was not complete without a dog, and a dog was scarcely complete without a man'. In 'The Letters of Sir Walter Scott' edited by H J C Grierson (1932-7) Vol. IV, Scott maintained that his larger dog Maida was a descendant of the Blue Spanish wolf-dog and the real deer grey-hound. He described Maida as about 6ft long from the tip of the nose to the tail, iron strong in proportion – was this perhaps the background to Byron's 'wolf dog'?

The year that Byron died, 1824, saw the founding of what is now known as the Royal Society of the Prevention of Cruelty to Animals, and it is not inconceivable that the writings and attitudes of both Byron and Scott gave impetus to its formation. Other animal legislation was to follow in the 19th century when bull-baiting was made illegal in 1835.

This book sets out to describe Byron's relationship with the many dogs which he owned in his lifetime.

CHAPTER I

# Boatswain The Eskimo Dog?

**'You're the very best dog in the Land'**

***Boatswain***
Oil on canvas, 1808
Clifton Tomson
(1775 – 1835)

Newstead Abbey,
Nottingham City Museums
and Galleries

*'I arose with the dawn, with my dog as my guide,*
*From mountain to mountain I bounded along.'*

From Byron's poem *'When I roved a young Highlander'*

Of the many dogs which Byron owned at one time or another during his lifetime, it is true that his two Newfoundlands held pride of place in his affections. The first, Boatswain, was to share his adolescent years in England while his second, Lyon (or Lion), was to be Byron's devoted companion on his fateful expedition to Greece some 16 years later, and was with him when he died at Missolonghi on 19th April 1824.

What then were the qualities and characteristics of the Newfoundland breed in general which seemed to find such favour in Byron's eyes? To answer this question we must take a look at the origins and development of the breed with particular reference to the early 19th century. A knowledgeable and contemporary source was the veterinary surgeon, William Youatt. His book entitled 'The Dog', first published in 1852, was sponsored by none other than John Cam Hobhouse (Lord Broughton, Byron's most durable and loyal friend, through Hobhouse's Chairmanship of the Committee of the 'Society for the Diffusion of Useful Knowledge'). Rather than use modern breed standards, Youatt's assessments of the various breeds of dogs which Byron owned will be drawn on extensively as he was a much respected practising vet in Byron's day.

Youatt states that the Newfoundland is a 'spaniel of large size' and 'a native of the island which bears his name'. But he has little good to say of the Newfoundlanders who he accuses of the gross maltreatment of 'so valuable an animal.' Apparently the dogs were used in winter for drawing very heavy loads of logs or pulling carts and 'were almost invariably urged and goaded on beyond their strength, fed only with putrid salt fish, and an inadequate quantity of even that. A great many of them are worn out and die before the winter is over; and when summer approaches and the fishing season commences many of them are quite abandoned and uniting with their companions prowl about preying on the neighbouring flocks or absolutely starving.'

The Author's copy of
**THE DOG**

By William Youatt,
London 1852

SPANIEL AND NEWFOUNDLAND DOGS.

THE NEWFOUNDLAND DOG.

However, Youatt presents a much happier picture of the breed in quoting from the 'Historical and Descriptive Sketches of British America' by J. Macgregor: 'In almost every other part of British America they are valuable and useful. They are remarkably docile and obedient to their masters… they are faithful, good-natured and ever friendly to man. They will defend their master and their master's property and suffer no person to injure either the one or the other and however extreme the danger they will not leave them for a minute. They seem only to want the faculty of speech in order to make their good wishes and feelings understood and they are capable of being trained for all the purposes for which every other variety of the canine species is used.'

Youatt also states that a prime recommendation for the Newfoundland is his fearlessness of water and that he had personally known of one dog which 'has preserved from drowning four human beings.' He also relates a number of case histories concerning the brave conduct of Newfoundlands in disasters at sea and cites examples illustrating the 'noble disposition' of these dogs.

Returning to the physical characteristics of the breed, Youatt's brief statement that they were 'spaniels of large size' seems odd as he goes on to describe a dog with little resemblance to what one would expect of the spaniel breed. So the term spaniel was applied in a much broader sense than it is today. The exact origins of the Newfoundland breed have never been proved. Some claim them to be the descendants of the black bear dogs allegedly imported into Newfoundland by the Norsemen around 1,000 A.D. On the other hand, it is more likely that the breed grew up through a series of crosses with mastiff and other types brought in by settlers and sailors from the 15th century onwards. Certainly Newfoundlands seem to have been fairly diverse in shape and size when they began to appear in Europe in the 18th century.

Youatt states that some of the 'true Newfoundland dogs' were brought to Europe 'and have been used as retrievers'. These, he says, 'were comparatively small but muscular, strong and generally black in colour.' Youatt claims that 'a larger variety has been bred and is now perfectly established. He is seldom used as a sporting dog or for draught but is admired on account of his stature and beauty and the different colours with which he is often marked.'

This larger strain appears to be the forerunner of the modern breed. Adult male dogs are sturdy and massive, weighing up to 150 pounds, but the 'different colours' referred to by Youatt no longer occur. There is a white-and-black 'Landseer' type – named after the famous royal painter who did much to popularise the breed in Victorian times – and occasionally bronze puppies are bred, but these are fairly rare in this country. Nor do the curly coats which were a feature of the breed 150 years ago appear today.

From the foregoing it is not difficult to imagine why Byron was particularly attracted to Newfoundlands. Complete devotion and loyalty were qualities that he would certainly have desired in a dog and it was these virtues which he was to extol from time to time in his cynical comparisons of dog and man. The Newfoundland's large size and noble mien would also have had a definite appeal to the young Byron, who was not averse, when opportunity offered, to 'cutting a figure' – and to be accompanied by a very large and obviously devoted dog would create a certain effect!

*Taking the biscuit*

***Princess Mary of Cambridge with Nelson, a Newfoundland dog*** (before June 1839)
Oil on canvas. Sir Edwin Landseer (1803 – 1873) Royal Collection © Her Majesty Queen Elizabeth II

Boatswain was the first of Byron's Newfoundlands and undoubtedly the best known of all his animals. Practically every biographer of Byron makes some mention of Boatswain. As Byron's letters show and his contemporaries relate, the mutual affection between dog and master was very great.

As to Boatswain's history, it is apparent from the epitaph on his tomb in the grounds of Byron's ancestral home Newstead Abbey, Nottinghamshire, that Byron believed him to have been born in Newfoundland in May 1803. Byron had him painted in his prime in 1808 – ironically, the year of his death – by Clifton Tomson (1775-1835), a Nottingham animal and sporting artist. The life-size painting still hangs today in Newstead Abbey. It is a simple yet striking portrait depicting the dog in a classical landscape setting. Something of his strength, proud bearing and gentleness is captured in the painting. He is predominantly black in colour but with a white 'collar' and 'socks'. His pricked ears (Newfoundlands' ears were and are normally pendent), general shape of his muzzle and texture of coat indicate some traces of a 'husky' dog type. Edward Jesse, another 19th-century writer on dogs in his book 'Anecdotes of Dogs' (1873) writes about the Esquimaux dog, 'it is muscular and broad-chested, his ears are pointed and in size about the height of the Newfoundland breed'.

*Brush with greatness*

Perhaps the most celebrated image of a Newfoundland dog. The black & white variety of the breed took its name from the artist, Landseer.

*A Distinguished Member of the Humane Society*
Oil on canvas
Sir Edwin Henry Landseer
(1802-1873), 1838

©Tate, London 2013

Boatswain is certainly less typical of the then more traditional Newfoundland than his much later successor, Lyon, who more closely resembles the painting by Ben Marshall of his young Newfoundland with his curly coat and pendent ears, dated 1811. Youatt also describes what he calls the Esquimaux dog from the north of North America used by the Esquimaux Indians often yoked to a sledge; they are big dogs, although not quite as massive as a Newfoundland and have pricked ears and a sharp muzzle. Today, such dogs usually go under the description of husky dogs. Youatt states that 'the Esquimaux is nearly the same as those from Newfoundland'. So it is easy to see why Byron thought Boatswain a Newfoundland when he was perhaps an Esquimaux dog.

There is no reliable record of how or when Byron acquired Boatswain, but accepting that he was born in 1803, it would certainly have been during the period when Mrs Byron and her son were living in Burgage Manor, Southwell, Nottinghamshire. In 1803, struggling with her finances, Mrs Byron had let Newstead Abbey to Lord Grey de Ruthyn for a period of five years and rented Burgage Manor in the small Georgian market town of Southwell, some 10 miles from Nottingham, from Mr E Falkner.

*Coach party*

*Burgage Manor & Green, with Byron & Boatswain*

Watercolour on paper
Nick Hugh McCann

© Nick Hugh McCann
Private Collection

During this period, the young Lord Byron – first at Harrow School and later at Trinity College, Cambridge – was in a state of almost continuous complaint and sometimes open rebellion against his mother's doubtless well-directed but shrill criticism of his carefree lifestyle and chronic overspending. He apparently resented every hour spent under her roof and affected to despise Southwell and its inhabitants as deadly dull, although in later years he was to see the town in a much more favourable light.

What Byron thought of Burgage Manor has been well documented.
On 2nd April 1804, writing to Augusta, he says: '(London) is preferable to this
horrid place, where I am oppressed with ennui, and have no amusement of any
Kind except the conversation of my mother which is sometimes very edifying
but not always very agreeable.  There are very few books of any Kind that are
either instructive or amusing, no society but old parsons and old Maids.'

Byron was exaggerating: the Manor had a well-stocked library...
By 1811, Byron's views about Southwell had mellowed.  In writing from
Newstead to his cousin R C Dallas, on 11th October, he said: 'now I know
a large village, or small town, about 12 miles off where your family would
have the advantage of very genteel society, without the hazard of being
annoyed by mercantile affluence where you would meet with men of
information and independence, and where I have friends to whom I shall
be proud to introduce you; There are, besides, a coffee-room, assemblies,
etc. etc; which bring people together.  My mother had a house there some
years, and I am well acquainted with the economy of Southwell, the name
of this little commonwealth.'

**Below:**
*A black & white issue*

A dog remarkably
similar to Boatswain.

*Newfoundland Dog*
Oil on canvas
Daniel Clowes
(1796 – 1828)

Grosvenor Museum, Chester

**Above:**
*Interested parties*

Further evidence perhaps that Byron's famous
friend was probably an 'Eskimo dog', or Husky.

***Exquimaux, Niger, Neptune***
Pencil & Watercolour
I.M. Joy (1843)
© HM The Queen

***Mad, Bad & Dangerous to Know***

***Lord Byron, miniature***
Artist unknown

Private Collection

Nevertheless, he enjoyed amicable relations with several Southwell families, particularly the Pigots who lived across the Green from the Manor. Their home became Byron's refuge from his mother's nagging. Elizabeth, the eldest daughter, several years his senior, was a sensible girl who encouraged Byron in his early writings and with whom he enjoyed an easy-going friendship without any of the amorous overtones which provoked much gossip among the parents of some other Southwell belles. During the holidays, the young people of Byron's circle engaged in amateur theatricals at the nearby house of the Leacroft family and had a good deal of fun – with Byron, as might be expected, the focal point of interest and action.

Boatswain came to be very well known in the little town as Byron's favourite, and accompanied him everywhere on his travels in the vicinity. He would probably have come into Byron's possession during the early 1800's (Byron thought 1803), but the first specific reference to him occurs in the summer of 1806 when Byron was down from Cambridge University for the summer vacation and visited his great friend of Harrow days, Edward Long, at Littlehampton in Sussex. Long's younger brother recorded that Byron stayed at the Dolphin Inn and that he brought with him his horses and his dog Boatswain.

Apparently, Byron spent his first day engaged in pistol-shooting practice on the beach, the targets being oyster shells by the pier. This account has an authentic ring and indeed is typical of the young Byron's flamboyant and eccentric style. Curiously enough, pistol shooting, which might have been considered as no more than a youthful fad, was to remain an activity which he practised assiduously throughout his life and in which he excelled. Few could beat him in hitting coins mounted on sticks or shattering bottle necks at 15 paces! It can be assumed that, given a Newfoundland's natural love of water, Boatswain would have thoroughly enjoyed his brief spell at the seaside. Indeed, young Henry Long recalled that, on at least one occasion, Boatswain leapt from the pier into the water, but that his brother's dog (somewhat inappropriately called Fish) could not be prevailed upon to follow suit. Although the so-called pier at Littlehampton was not one of those massive iron structures which proliferated around our shores in Victorian times, the drop into the water could have been 10 feet or more and therefore quite a daunting test for even a hardy water-bred dog. One can sympathise with the reluctance of poor Fish to emulate Boatswain's feat.

***Littlehampton Pier***
Oil on canvas
Augustus Wall Callcot, 1811-12

During the same summer vacation, Byron and John Pigot (Elizabeth's brother), then a medical student, paid a visit to Harrogate. After Byron's death, John Pigot – by then an eminent M.D. – gave an account of this visit to the Irish poet Thomas Moore when he was researching material for his famous biography of Byron published in 1830.

Apparently, the two youngsters travelled in style in Byron's own carriage drawn by post horses. Boatswain sat with Frank Boyce, Byron's valet, outside on the box. Byron also brought with him two of his saddle horses – Sultan and Brighton – who were in the charge of a groom, as was Byron's bull mastiff, Nelson. Nelson was a fine animal but extremely pugnacious and had to be kept muzzled for most of the time. He was also understandably very jealous of Boatswain. Byron and John Pigot lodged at the Crown Inn and although they took their meals in the public room, they had the use of a private sitting room. John Pigot complained that Byron used on occasions to have Nelson brought up to this room where he would wrestle and romp with him, throwing everything into disorder. He also related that when Boatswain and Nelson happened to meet, the most furious combat immediately ensued and that everyone available, including the waiters, was vigorously employed in attempting to part them. Usually this could only be affected by thrusting poker and tongs into the mouths of each.

All this must have enlivened life at the Crown, but worse was to follow. One day, Nelson escaped from the sitting room without his muzzle on and made for the stables, where he attacked a horse, seizing it by the throat. A stable boy roused the alarm and Frank, the valet, took one of Byron's pistols (which were always kept loaded in his room), ran out and shot Nelson through the head, 'to the great regret of Byron'. So the rivalry between these two great dogs, so different in temperament, ended tragically.

But it was not all dog fighting on that holiday in Harrogate. Byron and John Pigot were scribbling poetry and learning their parts for some amateur theatricals to be performed at Southwell later in the year, and John Pigot records in a letter to his sister, Elizabeth: '...There are many pleasant rides about here which I have taken in company with Boatswain, who, with Brighton, is universally admired...' To this Byron added a humorous addendum poking fun at John Pigot's laborious attempts at 'rhyming'.

Boatswain, despite the benign disposition attributed to Newfoundlands, was involved in frequent scrapes in Southwell, as exemplified by the following extract from a letter quoted in Thomas Moore's two-volume biography, 'Letters and Journals of Lord Byron with Notices of His Life', 1830. The writer is not named, but it is almost certainly Elizabeth Pigot, as she always spelled the shortened version of Boatswain's name as Bos'en: '...Bos'en has had another battle with Tippoo at the House of Correction and came off conqueror. Lord B brought Bos'en to our window this morning when Gilpin, who is almost always here got into an amazing fury ...' The House of Correction was close to Burgage Manor on Burgage Green.

Gilpin was a somewhat irascible fox terrier belonging to Mrs Byron and there was a constant and bitter feud between the two dogs, who had to be kept apart as much as possible. It would appear that Gilpin usually started the rumpus but had to be rescued from annihilation when Boatswain's temper was really aroused by his chivvying. There was, however, a happy ending to this feud. When Byron returned to Cambridge, leaving Boatswain at Southwell, Mrs Byron decided that it would be prudent to board Gilpin out with one of the tenant farmers at Newstead rather than face further confrontations between the two dogs in Byron's absence.

One day, Boatswain was found to be missing and – well-knowing Byron's rage if any harm should befall his beloved Newfoundland – a search was immediately instituted. Eventually, towards evening, Boatswain returned to Burgage Manor of his own accord, accompanied by little Gilpin, whom he shepherded straight to the kitchen fire before proceeding to lick him all over. It can only be deduced that Boatswain had missed his small persecutor and had made the long trek of many miles to Newstead with the express purpose of bringing him back. From then on all animosity between the two dogs ceased and it is said that thereafter Boatswain used to defend Gilpin against the insults of other dogs, running to his protection whenever he heard his bark.

The dogs of the two families were a source of mutual interest between Byron and Elizabeth Pigot and in a series of letters written to her from Cambridge and London during 1807, Boatswain and the other dogs receive frequent mention. Byron always adopted a facetious style in recounting or requesting news of Boatswain and the other dogs (who had to be left behind at Southwell for some of the time) and presumably Elizabeth replied in a similar jocular tone – although regrettably only two of her letters to Byron are still preserved. In one letter, Byron complained that his new bulldog puppy had 'grievously disturbed the gravity of old Boatswain who is seriously discomposed'. It is interesting that Byron should call Boatswain 'old' since he cannot then have been more than four years of age and in his prime – but the word is probably used here more as a term of endearment than signifying advanced years.

On another occasion, he enquired after Boatswain's health, referring to him as that 'Phoenix of canine quadrupeds'. He rarely failed to ask after the well-being of Elizabeth's dog 'the immortal Bran' (breed unknown) whom he also dubbed for good measure with typical Byronic irreverence as 'a count of the Holy Roman empire'. These animal drolleries were interlaced with racy gossip about personalities and riotous living at Cambridge where Byron affected to some purpose the lifestyle of a rakish young blood. Byron was disappointed that university rules prevented him from keeping his bulldog Smut in his college chambers, so he brought a tame bear, which he may have kept in a turret above his rooms – although he soon had to board him out in some stables in Ram Yard in the town!

**Lord Byron at 18**
Ink on card
William Leacroft,
Southwell

Private Collection

*W.S.L. Southwell.*

*Lord Byron*
*æt: 18.*

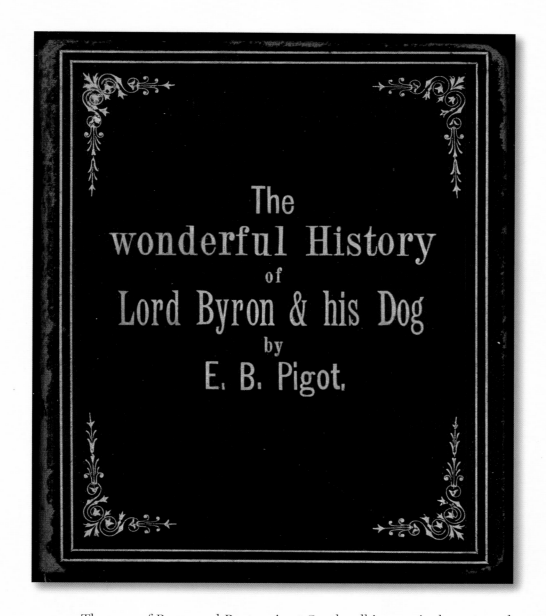

The saga of Byron and Boatswain at Southwell is amusingly portrayed in a little booklet written by Elizabeth. It is illustrated in watercolour (both Elizabeth and her mother were quite accomplished amateur artists) and provides a glimpse of the pleasant relationship between the three of them. The booklet, which is in the form of a poem parodying 'Old Mother Hubbard' now resides in the University of Austin, Texas, U.S.A. It is entitled '"The Wonderful History of Lord Byron & his Dog". Dedicated to that Right Honourable Infant the Lord Byron by his very obedient servant, the authoress EEP.' To my knowledge it is reproduced here in its entirety for the first time in colour.

*"The Wonderful History of Lord Byron & His Dog"*
Pencil, pen & watercolour on paper sketchbook
E. B. Pigot, Southwell, Notts, March 1807

The bookplate of Miriam Lutcher Stark

Elizabeth Pigot, holding her "Wonderful History", photographed in 1864, by T. Easter, Southwell

Below: the original manuscript's cover featuring her ink drawing of Byron's mermaid crest and the motto, 'crede Byron'

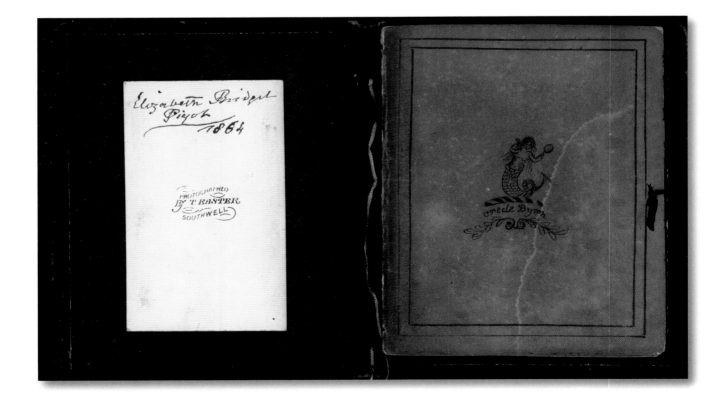

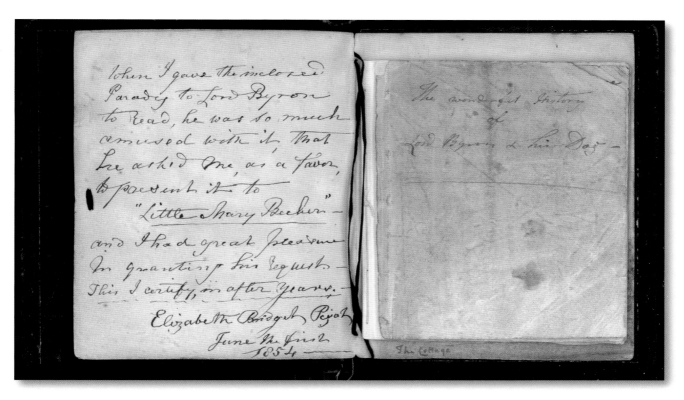

When I gave the inclosed Parody to Lord Byron to read, he was so much amused with it, that he asked me, as a favour, to present it to "Little Mary Beecher" - and I had great pleasure in granting his request - This I certify, in after years. Elizabeth Bridget Pigot June the first 1854.

[Dedi]cated to that Right Hon'ble infant the Lord Byron, By his very Humble Ser't: the Authoress

Every dog has his day.

The wonderful History of Lord Byron & his Dog -

Of Old Mother Hubbard no more shall be said,
She's weeping & wailing because his dog's dead.
Lord Byron's a person of fame and renown,
And his favourite Bo'sen's well known in the Town.

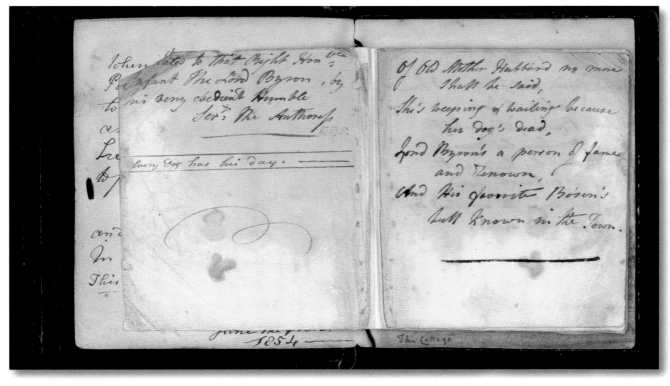

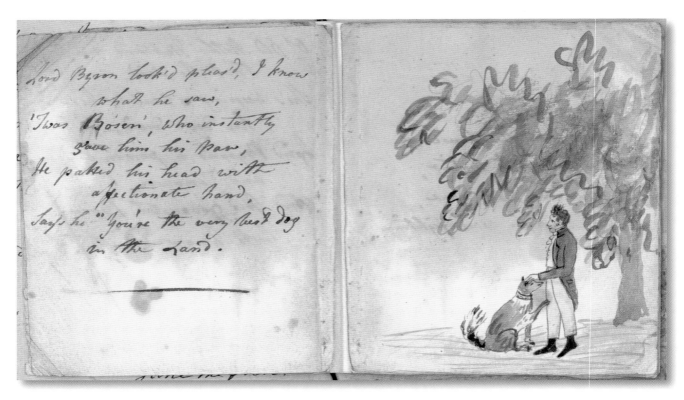

*Lord Byron look'd pleas'd, I know what he saw,*
*'Twas Bo'sen', who instantly gave him his paw,*
*He patted his head with affectionate hand,*
*Says he "You're the very best dog in the Land.*

*He went into the house & sat down to writing,*
*And when he had gone, found Bo'sen' was fighting.*

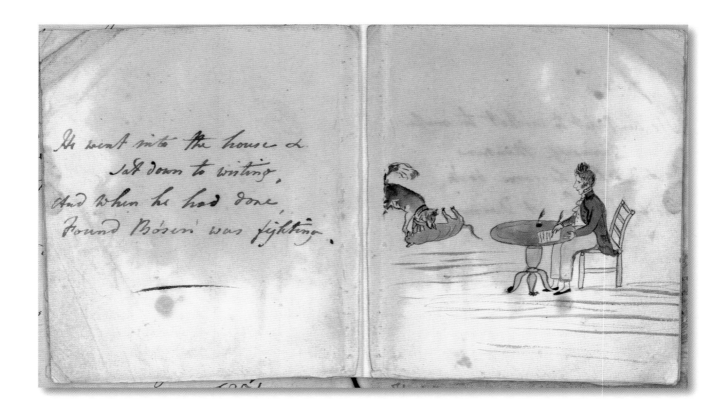

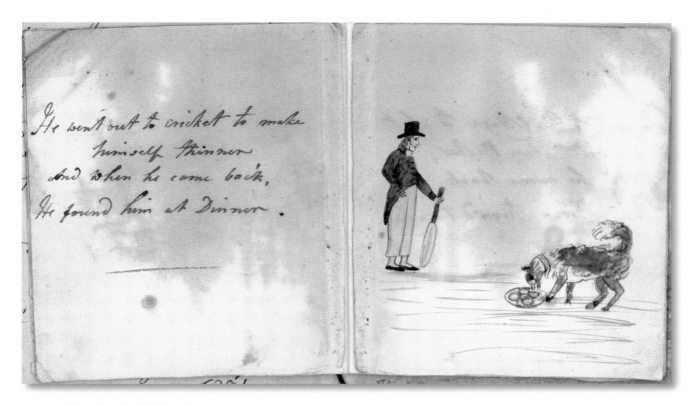

*He went out to cricket to make*
*    himself thinner*
*And when he came back,*
*    He found him at Dinner.*

*He went to the Cottage to chat*
*    with Ann Beecher,*
*& when he came back,*
*    Found Bo'sen' turn'd Preacher.*

*"Repent ye wicked, resist temptation."*

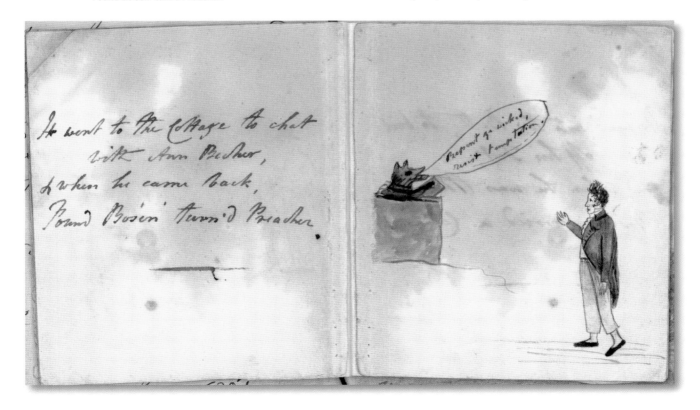

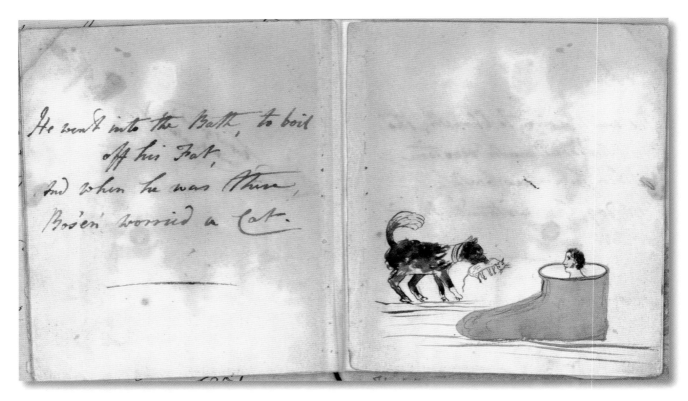

*He went into the Bath, to boil*
            *off his Fat,*
*And when he was there,*
            *Bo'sen' worried a Cat.*

*He went down to Church, tho'*
            *without much Devotion*
*& when he came back*
            *His dog lay without Motion.*

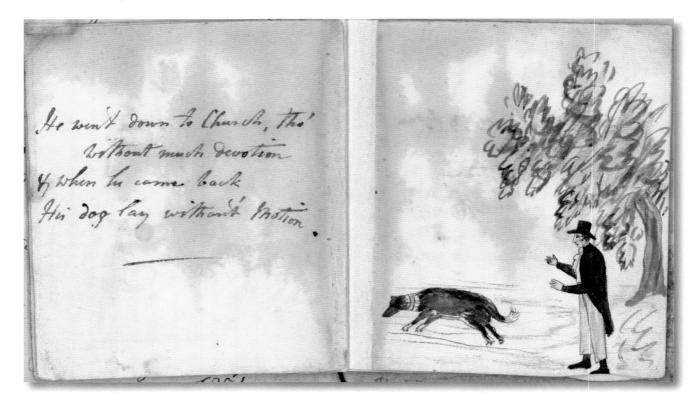

*He thought he was dead, & began*
*for to weep,*
*But in a short time,*
*He awoke from his Sleep.*

*He went to the Club to eat*
*Oysters with many,*
*and on his return,*
*Found him playing with*
*Fanny.*

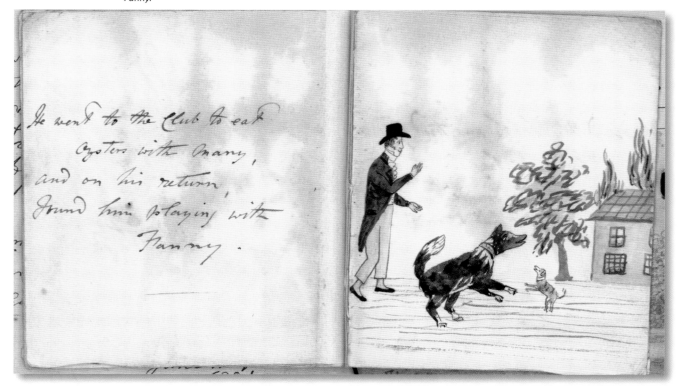

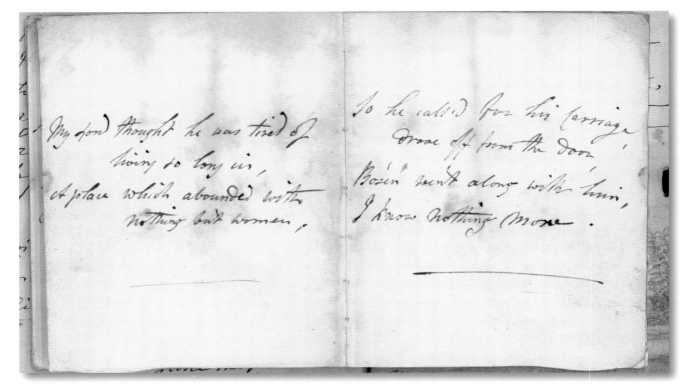

My Lord thought he was tired of living so long in,
A place which abounded with nothing but women,

So he call'd for his Carriage, drove off from the door,
Bo'sen' went along with him, I know nothing more.

Some sobb'd, some sighed & bitterly groan'd,
For the loss of this wonderful pair how they moan'd.
Poor Nanny & Betty were near sinking under,
And sharing the grave with his Lordship's dog Thunder.
But on weighing the matter with due Lamentation,
They thought it would be quite a loss to the nation.
So they took up his Book and drove away care,

with the Poems so moral they
found written there.

March 26th, 1807

*"Out upon Time! -
It for ever will leave,
but Enough of the past,
For the future to grieve."*

*The Cottage*

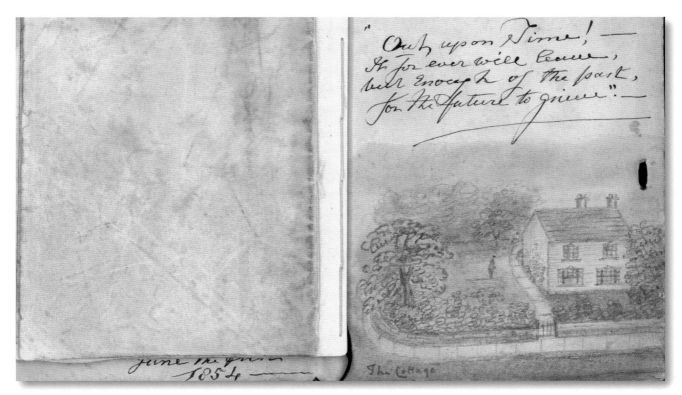

Although the parody features Boatswain and Byron's fondness for him, it also amusingly brings out some facets of Byron's character: a boyhood love of cricket; the need to slim (he was unfortunately prone to obesity and took violent and peculiar measures from time to time to cure it – in the autumn of 1806 he was 202 pounds, a great weight for someone 5ft 8½ins tall); religious scepticism (he went to church tho' without much devotion); riotous living (Boatswain preaching to him to repent and resist temptation); and the final little dig – Betty and her mother driving away care by reading Byron's 'so moral' poems. Whatever might be said about some of Byron's early poems written in those Southwell days, whether published or unpublished, they were certainly not paragons of morality if the complaints of certain Southwell fathers who felt their daughters' reputations had been compromised are to be believed!  As can be read in this excerpt from a poem 'To Mary' from his first privately printed volume of poems in 1806, 'Fugitive Pieces':

> *'Now, by my soul', 'tis most delight*
> *To view each other panting, dying,*
> *In love's extatic posture lying,*
> *Grateful to feeling, as to sight.'*

In 1808, Byron, having come down from Cambridge (he was later to be awarded his M.A. degree but never sat for any examinations) then occupied Newstead Abbey and at great cost renovated part of it. Boatswain accompanied him there (together with his tame bear and so-called wolf dog whose story is told later). It would have been a happy time for the great dog, as he could be with Byron continuously and was his favourite beyond any doubt. He could roam in the park-like acres surrounding Newstead Abbey and doubtless swim in the lake with his master, a most resolute and capable swimmer who was later to swim the Hellespont from Sestos to Abydos – a feat of which he was inordinately proud.

But before the end of 1808, Boatswain's life was to be brought to a hideous and untimely end. Apparently he was bitten by a rabid dog in Nottingham, contracted that dread disease and died in a state of madness in November 1808.

*Walking on Water*

*Ripley, a Newfoundland, owned by Kirsteen Farrar*

Photograph
Nick Hugh McCann

© Nick Hugh McCann

Rabies was rife in England at that time and the vet Youatt recounts many cases with which he had dealt. Although the symptoms were often difficult to detect in the early incubation period and did not always follow an entirely similar pattern, extreme restlessness, over-bright eyes, a change in the pitch of the voice and in eating habits, often accompanied by a voracious thirst, were pointers to the full development of the disease. The final stages were horrible in the extreme; the tongue enlarged and distorted, the mouth parched, with the dog desperate to drink but unable to. When in a fit, the chained animal would fly at any shadow or solid object or human being, seemingly impervious to restraint or pain and uttering the desolate howl which was a hallmark of the disease. Death when it came – usually within a few days of the severest symptoms setting in – was a merciful release, although of course, if the early signs were properly recognised (and they often were not) the dog would have been destroyed before the final stages were reached. Not all rabid dogs behaved so violently and Youatt tells a moving story of another Newfoundland which, although suffering from the full effects of the disease, remained tractable throughout, continued to offer his paw to be shaken and eventually died in the very act.

That Boatswain also died with dignity is related by Byron in a letter to his Cambridge friend Francis Hodgson, dated 18th November 1808: 'Boatswain is dead! He expired in a state of madness on the 10th, suffering much yet retaining all the gentleness of his nature to the last – never attempting to do the least injury to anyone near him – I have lost everything except old Murray...' Joe Murray was Byron's favourite Newstead servant.

It was extremely fortunate for Byron that Boatswain 'remained gentle to the end' for Thomas Moore, the poet, and Byron's first authentic biographer, relates that Byron was at first so ignorant of Boatswain's malady that, on several occasions, he wiped the saliva from the dog's mouth with his own hands. At this stage the risk of infection would have been very great and a speck of saliva entering a small cut, or worse still a bite, would have been enough. Although rather rough-and-ready remedies existed – the most effective apparently being the excising of the immediate area of the wound with 'caustic' (burning by nitric and other acids) – survival was certainly the exception rather than the rule. If Byron was actually aware of the risk, then his action was courageous to the point of foolhardiness.

Although there can be no doubting the sincerity and poignancy of Byron's immediate grief at the loss of his great favourite, it has to be said that Byron had a tendency to dramatise calamities of this kind. His mother was still alive at the time when he claimed that 'old Murray' was all he had left, although their relations were strained. When she died in 1811, Byron expressed similar sentiments – perhaps as a belated but dawning recognition of her sterling worth and devotion to his cause. And coupled, one might hope, with a twinge of conscience that he had never really made amends for his often thoughtless treatment of her.

In the immediate aftermath of Boatswain's death, Byron resolved that his tomb should be in the gardens of the Abbey and that a handsome memorial should be erected to mark the place of burial – something which he intended should be as close as possible to the original site of the high altar of the old Priory. That he missed his target by some hundreds of yards owes more to faulty surveying than any sudden conversion from extreme religious scepticism. But perhaps the greatest stir was caused by his expressly stated intention, to be embodied in a new will, that he should be buried alongside Boatswain's tomb under the same memorial plinth, and not in the family vault at nearby St Mary's Church, Hucknall. He engaged Samuel Bolton, a local solicitor, to draw up the will and, after exchanges of drafts and counter drafts, that clause in the will relating to his burial finally read as follows: '...I desire that my body may be buried in the vault of the garden of Newstead without any ceremony or burial service whatever and that no inscription save my name and age be written on the tomb or tablets; and that it is my will that my faithful dog may not be removed from the said vault. To the performance of this my particular desire I rely on the attention of my executors hereinafter named...'

These highly un-Christian burial arrangements and the sentiments so forthrightly expressed in the will clearly worried the worthy Samuel Bolton and he recommended to Byron that this clause be removed. But Byron was adamant and returned a haughty and brief reply that, 'It must stand'. After his mother's death in 1811 some changes in his will were necessary but again he refused to make any change in his burial arrangements. Events then not to be foreseen were ultimately to change everything and Byron's sale of Newstead Abbey in 1817 effectively put an end to this somewhat bizarre arrangement.

**Opposite:**
*Courting in the act*

A fanciful Victorian portrayal of the young Byron with his first love, Mary Chaworth of Annesley, accompanied by a very curly *Boatswain*.

Her successful suitor, Jack Musters, is seen riding towards them.

The distant village is Hucknall: after an extraordinary life Byron was eventually to be buried there in humble surroundings.

*Byron's Dream 1874*
Oil on canvas
Ford Madox Brown (1821-93)

*Manchester Art Gallery / The Bridgeman Art Library*

60

In due course, the handsome memorial plinth was erected over Boatswain's tomb with a slab inside of an appropriate size to support a human coffin. The plinth was inscribed with a prose epitaph and a poem – perhaps the most touching tribute ever penned by a man to his dog.

It is usually accepted that Byron composed both the epitaph and the poem, but there is clear evidence that John Cam Hobhouse actually composed the epitaph. The circumstances are amusing. Apparently Byron had discussed the proposed poem with Hobhouse who had suggested a

Near this Spot
are deposited the Remains of one,
who possessed Beauty without Vanity,
Strength without Insolence,
Courage without Ferocity,
and all the Virtues of Man without his Vices.
This Praise, which would be unmeaning Flattery
if inscribed over human Ashes,
is but a just tribute to the Memory of
BOATSWAIN, a DOG,
who was born in Newfoundland May 1803
and died at Newstead Nov.' 18th 1808.

When some proud Son of Man returns to Earth,
Unknown to Glory but upheld by Birth,
The sculptor's art exhausts the pomp of woe,
And storied urns record who rests below:
When all is done, upon the Tomb is seen
Not what he was, but what he should have been.
But the poor Dog, in life the firmest friend,
The first to welcome, foremost to defend,
Whose honest heart is still his Masters own,
Who labours, fights, lives, breaths for him alone,
Unhonour'd falls, unnotic'd all his worth,
Deny'd in heaven the Soul he held on earth:
While man, vain insect! hopes to be forgiven,
And claims himself a sole exclusive heaven.
Oh man! thou feeble tenant of an hour,
Debas'd by slavery, or corrupt by power,
Who knows thee well, must quit thee with disgust,
Degraded mass of animated dust!
Thy love is lust, thy friendship all a cheat,
Thy tongue hypocrisy, thy heart deceit,
By nature vile, ennobled but by name,
Each kindred brute might bid thee blush for shame.
Ye! who behold perchance this simple urn,
Pass on, it honours none you wish to mourn,
To mark a friend's remains these stones arise
I never knew but one — and here he lies.

*Tear jerker*

Perhaps the most moving and emotive tribute to a dog in the English language.

*Boatswain's epitaph*
Carved in Portland stone

**Opposite right:**
*'Bo'sen turn'd Preacher'*
Boatswain's 'dog' collar

**Opposite far right:**
*'His dog lay without Motion'*
Boatswain's tomb

Both to be seen at
Newstead Abbey,
Nottinghamshire

All pictures on these two pages:
Newstead Abbey,
Nottingham City Museums
and Galleries

slight rephrasing of the lines referring to the dog as his only friend. Byron humorously accused Hobhouse of being jealous of a dog and Hobhouse with his usual honesty admitted that he might be a little – 'But I can praise him in prose and match your misanthropy'. It was then agreed that Hobhouse should write the epitaph. This he did and it would certainly be difficult to better it. The lines of Byron's poem express his very strong feelings for the loss of his dog. 'The eulogy at the expense of folly and wickedness was a common 18th-century convention which he could have borrowed from his idolized Alexander Pope' (Leslie Marchand, 'Byron – a Biography', 1957).

Byron was to retain fond memories of Boatswain long after his death. On his return from Greece in 1811, when writing to Augusta Leigh from Newstead in one of his sombre moods, he states that he is glad that her spouse likes children 'as he will have to bring them up'. He goes on to say that for his part he likes nobody since he lost his Newfoundland dog, except his successor, a Dutch mastiff. In a letter to Thomas Moore of January 1815 containing some canine reflections, he refers to Boatswain as 'the dearest and alas the maddest of dogs'. 'Maddest' refers, of course, to the manner of his untimely death.

So ends the Boatswain saga. But he is remembered today both in Clifton Tomson's painting and his elegant memorial in the grounds of Newstead Abbey, Nottinghamshire. There is also a bronze statue of Byron by the sculptor Richard Belt at the southern end of Park Lane with Boatswain lying at his feet looking up at him. It was erected in 1880. In addition, a dog's brass collar with a saw-tooth upper edge flared out for protection (below) is retained at the Abbey and is said to be Boatswain's. In fact, Byron had a number of similar collars made for his dogs by a Mansfield firm and as they were not named individually there is no real proof that it was Boatswain's. So, whether Boatswain was a true Newfoundland or perhaps an Esquimaux dog, he remains one of the most loved and famous dogs in English literature.

**Pride and prejudice**

After Byron's death, Newstead (and Boatswain's tomb) became a place for romantic pilgrimage. In this wonderfully lyrical picture – painted the year after Byron's demise – folk are seen wandering about, doubtless reading racy extracts from his Lordship, and shedding a tear at his dog's epitaph; depicted here surrounded by flowers.

**Newstead Abbey**
Oil on canvas
Cornelius Varley,
1825

Government Art Collection

CHAPTER II

# Lyon The Wolf Dog

*There has been some confusion about Lyon, the so-called 'wolf dog', because Byron's second Newfoundland whose story is related in Chapter VI, bore the same name. But the two dogs' lives were separated by many years. This Lyon, like Boatswain, was with Byron in his adolescent years in England, while Lyon the second was probably the last dog he obtained in Italy before the Greek adventure – surviving his master at Missolonghi and dying in 1825.*

Certainly the best account we have of the first Lyon's character comes from Byron's own hand in some canine recollections contained in a letter to Thomas Moore, his poet friend, dated 19th January 1815. Moore had asked Byron whether he – 'the friend of the dog' – could say whether it was possible that any dog could recognise a master whom neither his own mother nor mistress could 'find out'. Apparently the question arose from Moore's reading of 'Roderick' by Robert Southey (Poet Laureate 1813), where such a situation was described. Byron penned a somewhat equivocal answer in the course of which is the following passage: 'But as for canine recollections as far as I could judge by a cur of mine own (always baiting Boatswain the dearest and alas the maddest of dogs) I had one (half a wolf by the 'she' side) that doted on me at 10 years old and very nearly ate me at 20. When I thought he was going to enact Argus, he bit away the backside of my breeches and never would consent to any sign of recognition in spite of all kinds of bones which I offered him...'

This is one of the most revealing passages Byron wrote about any of his animals and from it we may deduce that this dog, alleged by Byron to be half-wolf, was probably acquired shortly before Byron's 10th birthday (1798). According to Byron, he must have lived for at least a further 10 years – until some time after 1808. There is indeed proof of this from other sources.

In 1809, when Byron was at Falmouth waiting to board the Lisbon Packet at the start of his tour of the Levant, Mrs Byron was calculating the cost of attempting to run Newstead Abbey on a mere pittance. Among the many expenses with which she was saddled was the cost of feeding the wolf dog. She records that it cost £20 per annum for his food – a staggering amount – but presumably the long drawn-out French wars had led to inflation even in those days. In May 1810 we find Mrs Byron reminding John Hanson – Byron's dilatory but amiable lawyer and former guardian, of her enforced financial pinching and scraping to make ends meet and the need to economise by finding homes for two of Byron's dogs (unspecified) with tenant farmers on the Newstead estate. But according to the Byron scholar and author, Doris Langley Moore, the expensive wolf dog was still retained. This is perhaps scarcely surprising. It would certainly not have been easy to find a home for Lyon if, as Byron stated, he was likely to attempt to bite a hunk from one's backside! So if the direct and indirect evidence is to be believed, Lyon was still alive in 1810 at the ripe old age of at least 12.

It is evident from the foregoing that Lyon must have been acquired long before Boatswain and outlived him by several years, as Boatswain died at the end of 1808. He was not therefore obtained to be Boatswain's successor.

Although Byron grumbled retrospectively about Lyon's lack of affection for him and proved unable to bribe him, 'despite all kinds of bones', he evidently thought enough of him to have him painted by Clifton Tomson (probably at the same time as Boatswain, as the painting is dated 1808). The portrait depicts Lyon bestriding the Nottinghamshire landscape like some veritable colossus. From the painting, he was certainly a bizarre and fearsome-looking fellow, though not without a certain quaint appeal, if one cares for the unusual. His colouring was predominantly light brown with white 'socks' to the fore legs.

What credibility can be attached to Byron's claim that he was half wolf on the 'she' side? Clearly, the claim was not doubted by some and was even embellished by others. In lot 247, the catalogue of the abortive sale of Newstead Abbey in 1815 describes Clifton Tomson's depiction of Lyon succinctly and without hesitation as: 'A capital painting of a wolf dog in a carved gilt frame.' Though we may agree that it is indeed a 'capital' painting, there seems to be a rather matter-of-fact inference that other paintings of wolf dogs were frequently to be met with, but were altogether less capital! One of Byron's closest Cambridge friends, Charles Skinner Matthews – in an amusing and oft-quoted letter to his sister, written 22nd May 1809 after visiting Byron at Newstead – describes the curious regime there and the hazards of entry: '...But have a care how you proceed; be mindful to go there in broad daylight and with your eyes about you for, should you make any blunder, - should you go to the right of the hall steps, you are laid hold of by a bear, and, should you go to the left, your case is still worse, for you run full against a wolf!'

**_Poet and  the Wolf_**

**_Lyon, The Wolf Dog_**

Oil on canvas
Clifton Tomson
(1775 − 1828), 1808

Newstead Abbey,
Nottingham City Museums
and Galleries

Later in the same letter, when describing the daily and nightly sports, he refers to 'playing with the bear, or teazing the wolf.' Now there is not the slightest doubt that Matthews was referring to Lyon, but from wolf dog he has now progressed to a full-blown wolf. Doubtless Matthews' remarks were meant as a jest to amuse and pleasantly shock his sister (he had something of a reputation as a wit) but they have tended to gain credibility with the passage of time, and today the casual Byron acquaintance accepts that he kept a wolf and bear. After all, if a bear why not a wolf?

It is worth noting that Byron called Lyon a cur ('a cur of mine own'). Youatt describes a cur as a sheep dog crossed with a terrier and that 'somewhat deservedly he has obtained a very bad name as a bully and coward'. But the term is probably common to any cross-bred dog of surly or churlish disposition.

Apart then from Byron's own assertion, the only other clue to a possible part-wolf ancestry must rest on Clifton Tomson's painting. The carriage of the tail and long facial region are wolf-like. On the other hand, Lyon's eyes are those of a dog. The wolf has elliptical-shaped pupils while those of the dog are round. Dogs have been crossed with wolves over many centuries, and probably husky types more so than any other. It is therefore by no means impossible – though of course not proven on the evidence available – that Lyon may have had wolf blood in his veins. If so, it probably stemmed from several generations back.

The most commonly-held rationalisation of Lyon's type is that he was simply an 'Alsatian'. Any breeder of Alsatians – or German shepherd dogs to give them their correct title – would be horrified to hear Lyon dubbed as one of their breed. In fact, Alsatians did not come into existence until late in the 19th century, through the careful crossing of two distinct types of German sheep-herding dogs. Nor was Lyon a wolf dog in the sense that he might have been a specific type of dog used to protect sheep or cattle against wolves. Youatt describes one such breed of dog as the 'Italian or Pomeranian wolf dog' and says that two were brought to the Zoological Society in 1833, 'and they remain there an ornament to the gardens.' They certainly bore no resemblance to Lyon, and Youatt was of the opinion that they appeared too gentle 'to contend with so powerful and ferocious an animal as the wolf.' So Lyon's immediate ancestry must remain something of a mystery. He would, however, appear to have at least some of the basic characteristics (if one ignores the tail) of the old European shepherd dogs – of which there were many strains – and the possibility of an earlier wolf cross remains credible.

There is no factual evidence as to exactly when Lyon died, but he is not referred to after Byron returned from his Levant tour in 1811, so it would probably have been about this time. In any case, he would have been very old by then. He seems to have given rather less than complete devotion to his master and this would certainly have irritated Byron, who liked and expected affection from his dogs. But he was honest enough to admit that even 'bone bribery' had failed in this case. Like that of Boatswain the Newfoundland, Lyon's portrait is also hanging at Newstead Abbey.

*Thro' thy battlements, Newstead,*
*the hollow winds whistle;*
*Thou, the hall of my fathers,*
*art gone to decay.*

### Welcome to the Pleasure Dome

Newstead Abbey has had a fascinating history: founded as a priory by Henry II c. 1163 – one of many penances he paid following the murder of Thomas Becket – and sacked by Henry VIII during the Dissolution of the Monasteries.

In 1540 the Abbey was granted to Sir John Byron of Colwick who began its conversion into a country house. William Byron, the 5th Baron, known as 'The Wicked Lord', kept the house as a pleasure dome, adding follies and forts and using them for mock battles with lifesize ships and cannons! His excesses led to the ruin of the estate, which the poet Byron inherited on the death of the 5th Baron in 1798.

Byron sold the Abbey to his Harrow schoolfriend, Thomas Wildman, who improved the fabric of the building and interiors. In 1861 William Webb, the African explorer, bought it and since his day, it has remained largely unaltered. Newstead Abbey is now owned and run as a heritage attraction by Nottingham City Council to whom it was given in 1931 by the philanthropist Sir Julien Cahn.

### Newstead Abbey from the air

©Nick Hugh McCann

*Short back and sides*

*Les tondeuses de chiens*
*(Dog cleaners)*
*Twenty-four subjects exhibiting*
*the Costume of Paris*
Hand-coloured lithograph
Pub. John Johnston, 1820

'Designed & drawn on Stone
by J.J. Chalon'

Designed & drawn on Stone by J.J. Chalon.  1820

S TONDEUSES DE CHIENS.

CHAPTER III

# The Bulldogs

'To frighten them into capitulation;
A phantasy which sometimes seizes warriors,
Unless they are game as Bull-dogs and Fox-terriers'

*Don Juan* Canto VII verse 24

*Grrrr*
No guessing who is the boss here

*Alexander and Diogenes*
Oil on canvas
Sir Edwin Henry Landseer (1802-1873)
Exhibited 1848

The bulldog's medieval ancestor was probably the Alaunt – a mastiff-like animal used by butchers to herd oxen and cattle. Over many centuries, the old English bulldog came to be recognised as the epitome of courage, tenacity and endurance. The English as a race have been proud to be identified with these bulldog characteristics – as typified by rugged 'John Bull' of the political and humorous cartoon with his faithful bulldog at his side.

The bulldog of Byron's day had few of the amiable qualities of his present-day descendants. Our forebears bred and trained him for the prime purpose of baiting the bull and the bear, and even matched him with lions and other wild beasts. It is perhaps hard to believe that these degrading and barbarous practices were not legally abolished by Act of Parliament until 1835, and then only after a spirited defence of these 'manly' sports!

*Fair Play?*

*Bull baiting*
Henry Thomas Alken
(1785 – 1851)
Published by Thomas McLean,
1820 (print)

Private Collection /
The Stapleton Collection /
The Bridgeman Art Library

Although William Youatt's contemporary description of the bulldog and his pugnacity may seem exaggerated when one considers the present benevolent qualities of the breed, he is essentially accurate in his basic facts: 'The round, thick head, turned up nose and pendulous lips of this dog are familiar to us all, while his ferocity makes him in the highest degree dangerous. In general he makes a silent although ferocious attack and the persisting powers of his teeth and jaws enable him to keep his hold against any but the greatest efforts, so that the utmost mischief is likely to ensue as well to the innocent visitor as to the ferocious intruder. The bulldog is scarcely capable of any education and is fitted for nothing except ferocity and combat.

'The name of this dog is derived from his being too often employed until a few years ago in baiting the bull. It was practised by the low and dissolute in many parts of the country. Dogs were bred and trained for this purpose, and while many of them were injured or destroyed, the head of the bull was lacerated in a most barbarous manner. Nothing can surpass the fury with which the bulldog rushed on his foe and the obstinacy with which he maintained his hold. He fastened upon the lip, the muzzle or the eye and there hung in spite of every effort of the bull to free himself from his antagonist.'

It is quite true that bull-baiting dogs were trained always to attack the head of the bull, which was tethered by a few yards of stout rope to a stake, which could revolve and thus allow the bull to face his adversary. The aim of the bulldog or dogs was to pin the bull by his nose to the ground. Dogs which attacked the bull's flanks were considered cowardly and thrown out. Bulls could, and frequently did, toss dogs 30 or more feet into the air and, horribly gashed or with broken limbs, a staunch bulldog would persistently return to the attack while breath remained in him, urged on by his master intent on redeeming his wager.

A print engraved by Henry Thomas Alken gives a presumably realistic impression of a 'bait' with the two attacking dogs being well and truly tossed by the bull. Another picture shows dogs attacking a bull in the early stages of a Spanish bullfight, c. 1787.

Bulldogs were also used for dog fighting in the 'pit' (the arena for battle) where individual dogs were matched against one another for wagers. By the end of the 18th century this was a popular 'sport' among all classes (as was terriers killing rats), but curiously enough it led to the gradual demise of the pure-bred fighting bulldog because bulldogs crossed with terriers proved more adept and successful fighters in the pit. These were the progenitors of the present day bull terrier. From all this brutality and pugnacity the bulldog emerges with credit – his masters with none.

After Newfoundlands, Byron seems to have had a particular liking for bulldogs. It is possible to identify by name at least three which he owned and there may well have been others. Byron was a great admirer of physical courage and tenacity and these attributes in a dog would certainly have appealed to him – especially that element of fearless courage which drove the bulldog to fight to the death any adversary regardless of size or strength. But there is perhaps a contradiction here – as there is in so many of Byron's actions. Byron on numerous occasions showed himself to be compassionate to a degree well beyond the times in which he lived and it is difficult to believe that he would have encouraged or taken part in a bull bait. Nevertheless, in writing to John Murray, his publisher, from Italy on 1st August 1819, he attempts to reassure him that he will defend himself against the many literary critics of 'Don Juan' by using the analogy of a bull bait: 'Don't be alarmed – you will see me defend myself gaily – that is – if I happen to be in Spirits – and by Spirits I don't mean your meaning of the word – but the spirit of a bulldog when pinched – or a bull when pinned – it is then they make best sport – and as my Sensations under an attack are probably a happy compound of the united energies of those amiable animals – you may perhaps see what Marral calls "rare sport" – and some good tossing and goring in the course of the controversy...' This certainly seems to imply actual experience of the 'sport'.

It is most likely that Byron's active interest in bull baiting would have begun and ended during his student days at Cambridge, when he was avid for new experiences. In July 1809, when travelling through Spain, Byron and his friend John Cam Hobhouse went to see a bullfight at Puerta Santa Maria near Cadiz in the very south of Spain. Byron was disgusted with the brutality of the performance, being particularly revolted by the 'wild plunging of the tortured horse'. Byron devoted several verses of his poem 'Childe Harold' (1812) to a description of the bullfight – here is one of the verses:

*Foil'd, bleeding, breathless, furious to the last,*
*Full in the centre stands the bull at bay,*
*Mid wounds, and clinging darts, and lances brast,*
*And foes disabled in the brutal fray:*
*And now the Matadores around him play,*
*Shake the red cloak, and poise the ready brand:*
*Once more through all he bursts his thundering way -*
*Vain rage! The mantle quits the conynge hand,*
*Wraps his fierce eye – 'tis past – he sinks upon the sand!*

**Below:**
*Horns of a dilemma*

*Colección de las principales suertes de una corrida de toros (Collection of the main actions in a bullfight)*
Hand-coloured etching
Print made by Antonio Carnicero, 1787-1790

Sir Walter Scott, a good friend of Byron, and a warm friend of dogs, said that 'The cleverest dog I ever had was what was called a bull-dog terrier.' Byron's correspondence with Elizabeth Pigot of Southwell of which the circumstances are recorded in the previous chapter, provides us with information on two bulldogs he acquired while at Cambridge.

# SAVAGE

On 11th June 1807, in a letter to Elizabeth, he reports the acquisition of a bulldog puppy called Savage. Byron avers that while he was not a thoroughbred (perhaps a terrier cross) he is 'the finest puppy I have ever saw and will answer much better.' Savage was the pup who had 'grievously discomposed the gravity of old Boatswain.' He had also bitten Byron's fingers for good measure. Elizabeth appears to have acted as an intermediary in procuring Savage and Byron asks her to find out the cost, expenses, etc so that he can reimburse a 'Mr G...' who has not been identified. In the same letter, Byron facetiously opines that Savage 'ought to be immortal' (a phrase he used often in jest in his correspondence with Elizabeth when alluding to their dogs as if they were imbued with the power of mythological gods). However, his extravagant hope was all too soon to be dashed, as in writing to Elizabeth only a few weeks later, on 30th June, he tells the sad news that Savage has died, adding with his typical self-deflating cynicism that 'Flesh both of cur and man is grass.' It is not known what disease claimed him so early in life but puppy mortality, as with human babies, was exceedingly high in those days. It may have been distemper or enteritis – both killer infections. At least Savage has a name to be remembered by, which is more than can be said about many other Byron dogs.

# SMUT

Byron was obviously determined to succeed in his quest for a bulldog, and by early August he had made good the loss of Savage and had purchased another bulldog. This one he claimed was a thoroughbred. Again he obviously hoped much of him and, in writing to Elizabeth, stated that he was 'worthy to be the co-adjutor of the aforesaid celestials.' These celestials were none other than Elizabeth's dog Bran, and of course, that 'Phoenix of canine quadrupeds', Boatswain. After these superlatives it comes as something of an anti-climax (and doubtless Byron intended it as such) to learn that his name was Smut! Alas, there is no further direct reference to Smut in Byron's later correspondence, but if he survived for any length of time he would almost certainly have gone to Newstead Abbey in 1808, when Byron came down from Trinity College, Cambridge. He would therefore have been one of several animals which Mrs Byron struggled to maintain as temporary chatelaine of the Abbey during Byron's absence on his tour of Greece and the Levant from 1809 to 1811.

# MORETTO

After Smut, a good many years were to elapse before another identifiable bulldog claimed attention.

After leaving England in April 1816, Byron was to lead a peripatetic existence in various provinces and towns of what today is Italy, but which then was a collection of principalities mostly under the Suzerainty of Austria. He collected about him wherever he lived a kaleidoscope of amours, friends, acquaintances – and, by no means least – dogs and other animals.

According to Shelley's account of a visit he paid to Byron in 1820, when Byron was living with his mistress Teresa Guiccioli at the Guiccioli Palazzo in Ravenna, he was astonished at the number of different animals (a veritable menagerie) which Byron had collected about him. Writing to Thomas Love Peacock in August 1821, Shelley had listed the animals in Byron's possession: 'Ten horses, eight enormous dogs, three monkeys, five cats, an eagle, a crow, and a falcon, five peacocks, two guinea hens and an Egyptian crane; and all of these, except the horses, walk about the house, which every now and then resounds with their unarbitrated quarrels, as if they were masters of it.'

Among these would have been his bulldog called Moretto, who was probably acquired at least a year or so previously. In fact, Moretto is specifically mentioned by Byron when writing to Richard Hoppner from Venice 25th October 1819. Byron bemoans the fact that 'all my household staff have the fever, except Fletcher, Allegra and Mysen (as we used to say in Nottinghamshire) and the horses and Mutz – and Moretto...'

Byron wrote to his publisher John Murray from Venice on 25th May 1819 asking for his usual domestic needs: 'I petition for toothbrushes – powder – Magnesia - Macassor oil – I want besides a Bulldog – a terrier – and two Newfoundland dogs'. Quite how Byron thought Murray could supply such a number of dogs is puzzling. Yet Murray writes to Byron in January 1820, 'Captain Fyler has been with me and will positively fulfill your commission about dogs – I bought a Capital Bull Dog for you and after paying for his feed for 4 months I got the man to take him back thinking – as you never renewed your order on this subject to me that you mentioned it in joke.' In a letter to Murray from Ravenna on 21st February 1820, Byron writes to Murray, 'The Bulldogs will be very agreeable – I have only those of this country which though good and ready to fly at anything – yet have not the tenacity of tooth and stoicism in endurance of my canine fellow citizens – then pray send them by the readiest conveyance perhaps by sea...'

In a later letter to Murray, of 1st March 1820, Byron refers to domestic wants which include: '...the bulldogs – magnesia – soda powders – toothpowder – brushes and everything of the kind which are here unobtainable...' The bulldogs were still required and some of his requirements did turn up eventually – but there is no confirmation of the arrival of the dogs and the presumption must be that they were probably never sent.

It would therefore seem reasonably certain that Moretto would have been one of the Italian tribe, though apart from their alleged lack of 'tenacity of tooth and endurance', their characteristics do not appear to have differed greatly from Byron's 'canine fellow citizens.' It is interesting that Byron corroborates Youatt's view of the formidable fighting qualities of the English dog. Nevertheless, that Moretto was 'ready to fly at anything' was convincingly demonstrated when, while living in the villa Lanfranchi near Pisa in 1822, Byron was joined by Leigh Hunt, the radical writer and poet, along with Hunt's pregnant wife and six children. Moretto promptly attacked the Hunts' pet nanny goat which had accompanied the family from England as a portable source of milk, biting an ear off the wretched animal.

Relations were further strained on the domestic front by the general grubbiness and indiscipline of the Hunt children, whom Byron likened with gusto and fair accuracy to a band of 'yahoos'. Henceforth, Moretto was to be employed in protecting his master's apartments – by growls or worse – from the intended ravages of these youthful yahoos, and indeed from other prospective visitors of greater repute. Thomas Medwin, when he visited Byron with Shelley in November 1821, came face to face with 'the English Bulldog', but was considerably relieved that he appeared to know Shelley and let them pass with no more than a growl. Medwin published a book, 'Conversations of Lord Byron', in 1824 and it was a great success, going to 15 editions between 1824 and 1842 and extending Byron's influence in Europe. The last sentence in Medwin's book states: 'Certain it is, that a nation who may well pride herself on so many great sons, will place Byron, all radiant as he is, by the side of those who have done most honour to her name!'

As to the literary partnership between Byron and Hunt which was the basis for the arrival of the whole Hunt family, this was to prove as prickly and unrewarding as their social and domestic contacts.

At this period, Moretto's aggressive tendencies are further revealed by an entry in the account book of Lega Zambelli, Byron's steward (formerly in the employ of Count Guiccioli, husband of Byron's mistress Teresa), who records the purchase of wine for the treatment of 'Medoro bitten by Moretto.' Wine was often used as an antiseptic.

Although Byron disposed of many of his animals when he left Ravenna for Pisa, Moretto was retained – probably because Byron valued his deterrent capabilities. Despite his affrays at Pisa, which one suspects may have amused rather than dismayed Byron, Moretto moved with Byron in October 1822 to Albaro near Genoa, to live in Casa Saluzzo, where Lyon the Newfoundland was acquired. Like Lyon, Moretto was chosen to accompany the expedition to Greece. It is recorded that he sailed in the Bombard with Pietro Gamba, doubtless to act as guard to the expedition's main baggage, supplies and arms which were transported in that rather cumbersome vessel. After capture by a Turkish warship and subsequent fortuitous release, the Bombard reached Missolonghi on the 4th January 1824.

There would certainly have been plenty of useful work for Moretto to do in guarding Byron's quarters and possessions at Missolonghi, with much coming and going of the Suliote guards billeted nearby, as well as a constant stream of visitors of various nationalities. If previous experience is any guide, one might imagine that Moretto, given his proclivity for 'flying at anything' could well have been involved in a fracas or two in the propitious circumstances which then existed at Missolonghi. But if Moretto took an ear of a surly Suliote irregular or a devious patriot, or even sank his teeth into a local tradesman, there was no Lega Zambelli to record it.

There remains the intriguing question of Moretto's disposal after Byron's death. Was he one of the three dogs which John Cam Hobhouse observed playing on the deck of the Florida as she brought Byron's body home? It is known that Lyon was certainly one, and that he was subsequently given to Hobhouse to care for. Doris Langley Moore states that the two other dogs were given to Henry Drury, Byron's tutor at Harrow School and later his great friend. Unfortunately, the dogs received by Henry Drury are not named, but it would indeed have been a fitting and a just reward for his long and faithful – if somewhat tempestuous – service to Byron, if Moretto could have ended his career in the peaceful Harrow scene of the 1820s. Whatever Moretto's end, he was clearly something of a character and his actions bear out at least some of the characteristics of bulldogs of that era as described by the vet Youatt.

THE BULL-DOG.

CHAPTER IV

# Mutz or 'Short Tail'

*Mutz was acquired in the rather impulsive way in which Byron seems to have obtained many of his animals. He saw him when travelling between Berne and Fribourg, liked him because he appeared to be tres mechant and bought him there and then from his doubtless somewhat surprised, but apparently satisfied, owner. The sum offered, if experience is any guide, was probably a good one because Byron was never mean over this kind of deal.*

The actual circumstances of the purchase of Mutz are revealed in a diary that Byron kept from 17th September 1816 to the 28th of that month in 1816. He had then been in Europe for only a few months following the break-up of his marriage to Annabella Milbanke. His 'Alpine Journal', as he called it, was intended for his beloved half-sister, Augusta Leigh. He was accompanied on this Alpine excursion by his old friend John Cam Hobhouse who had also been with him on part of his Levant tour undertaken a few years earlier.

The entry in his journal for 26th September records his journey from Berne to Fribourg. He first mentions passing a battlefield where the Swiss, he says, had managed to beat the French in one of the late wars against the French Republic. Then, with a typically rapid Byronic switch of subject, he recounts his purchase of Mutz: 'Bought a dog – a very ugly dog – but tres mechant. This was his great recommendation in his owner's eyes and mine – for I mean him to watch the carriage – he hath no tail and is called "Mutz" which signifies "Short tail" – he is apparently of the Shepherd dog genus!'

Byron does not appear to have brought any dogs with him from England and – as he had already clattered for several hundreds of miles across Europe in his costly and cumbersome replica of Napoleon's coach, and would have experienced something of the hazards of journeying on the continent in those lawless times – it is perhaps not surprising that he was on the lookout for a good guard dog.

From Byron's amusing description of him, is there any breed of dog extant – then or now – to which Mutz might conceivably be allocated? At the time, there were many different regional types of shepherd and cattle drovers' dogs in Germany and Switzerland. There seems to be at least a possibility, however, that Mutz may have been one of the large, tough, Swiss dairymen's or butchers' dogs used for herding cattle in Baden and Württemburg, from which the modern Rottweiler breed has been developed. It is alleged that these Swiss drovers' dogs were originally descended from the fierce and powerful animals used by the Swabian knights to hunt wild boar.

Despite his tres mechant characteristics, that Mutz must have been both tractable and trainable is demonstrated in a letter to Augusta Leigh dated 6th November 1816, where Byron adds a postscript: 'I forgot to tell you that my dog (Mutz by name and Swiss by nation) shuts a door when he is told – there – that's more than Tip can do.'

Tip was Augusta's dog, breed unspecified. Byron once described a pig he had seen to be 'as hideous as Tip', so clearly he was no beauty. His letters to Augusta are full of amusing asides and detail of the kind exemplified in the postscript quoted above, with snippets of information about his animals and other pets. In turn, he also sought news from her concerning her 'rabbit warren of a family'.

On 22nd April 1817, in a letter from Florence to John Cam Hobhouse penned while travelling to Rome to meet his friend there, Byron relates the story of Mutz's mountain encounter with a 'moderate-sized Pig'. At this time, Mutz was clearly still in favour as coach guard and travelling companion: 'Mutz is here – he was promoted into a Bear in the natural History of the Bolognese (who might have learned better at the Institute) a character which he has by no means sustained in point of valour – he having been defeated with loss of honour – hair – and almost the small remains of a tail which the Docker had left him – by a moderate-sized Pig on the top of the Pennine Alps – the Pig was first thrown into confusion and compelled to retire in great disorder over a steep stone wall but somehow he faced about in a damned hollow way or defile and drove Mutz from all his positions – with such slaughter that nothing but night prevented a total defeat...'

Poor Mutz! A hog, whether wild or partially so, could be an extremely tough customer for a solo dog to tackle, and his boar-hunting ancestors would have hunted in packs. However, Mutz clearly lost face (as well as hair) from his defeat by this 'moderate-sized pig' and probably some of his swagger too!

At any rate, Byron seems to have been amused by this notable encounter and its unexpected outcome, and Mutz remained with him for several more years during his travels through Italy. There is news of Mutz again in April 1819 when Byron, writing to John Cam Hobhouse, refers to several different animals in his 'menagerie' and states that, 'Mutz is still in high old age'. He would then have been with Byron for nearly three years and this indicates that he was already a mature dog when purchased in 1816 – if 'high old age' has any literal meaning.

Mutz was still alive and with the Byron entourage at Ravenna in autumn of 1821 when Byron decided to move to Pisa to be near his poet friend, Shelley. Unfortunately, the move was a complicated one as, while living with Teresa at the Palazzo, he had amassed not only chattels but a menagerie of diverse animals and birds. Byron felt obliged to part with a number of his pets and he entrusted them to his pliable banker in Ravenna, one Pellegrino Ghigi. According to a deposition made by Ghigi to the executors of Byron's estate, included in the list of those animals and birds left behind in his care was 'a peasant dog'. This dog was probably Mutz, now well advanced in years. Byron probably felt that, of the dogs, he was least able to move on to further adventures. Byron's actions may seem callous but it seems probable that at the time he saw Ghigi as no more than a temporary custodian of his surplus pets and that at some point in the future he hoped to re-claim them. However, as we know, events were to prove otherwise.

**Rather you than me...**

***The Mastiff***
Watercolour on paper
Sydenham Teast Edwards
(*c.*1768-1819)

THE MASTIFF.

CHAPTER V

# The Mastiffs

*Although it has already been said that Byron had a particular liking for the Newfoundland and bulldog breeds, there is evidence to show that he probably owned more dogs of the mastiff type during his life than any other. The word 'type' is used advisedly because there was a tendency in the past, before breeds came to be established and recognised by certain well-defined criteria, to refer to any very large, powerfully-built guard dog which did not fit easily into any other classification as a 'mastiff'.*

In fact, the mastiff breed is one of great antiquity and probably Britain's oldest. Youatt states, 'It is probable that the mastiff is an original breed peculiar to the British islands.' Modern scholars would contest this statement. The mastiff is usually credited with being descended from the huge warrior dogs of Epirus, trained for and used effectively by the Mollossi people in battle. It is not clear how their descendants found their way to these Isles. They may have been brought here by Mediterranean merchants engaged in the tin trade or perhaps through our early trade links with the peoples of the low countries.

By the late Anglo-Saxon era, we find that the mastiff had become something of an all-purpose dog capable of hunting as well as guarding. They may have been the dogs referred to by chroniclers of the day as 'big dunne coloured hounds'.

The strict forest laws which were applied throughout the Middle Ages fell particularly heavily on the mastiff, a dog large and powerful enough to pull down a deer. Mastiffs kept within the confines of the forest were

subject to the law of 'expeditation'. This was the compulsory maiming of a
 dog so that it could not hunt deer. A common method was to cut off three
toes from the right front foot. This barbarous practice was still the law
until the reign of James I.

In Byron's time, the mastiff and his first cousin the bull mastiff, seemed
to have settled firmly into the role of canine night watchmen. Youatt describes
the mastiff as having 'a grave and somewhat sullen countenance and his deep
toned bark is often heard during the night... and in the night especially he
watches the abode of his master with the completest vigilance. In fact, nothing
would tempt him to betray the confidence which is reposed in him.'

The first of Byron's mastiff types which can be positively identified
by name and description is the ill-fated Nelson. According to Dr John Pigot
– who recounted Nelson's terrible fights with Boatswain when Byron and he
spent a week or two at the Crown Inn, Harrogate, in the summer of 1806 –
Nelson was a bull mastiff: 'beautifully formed but very ferocious'. This
episode, and its tragic dénouement – when Nelson escaped unmuzzled,
attacked a horse in the stables and was shot dead by Frank Boyce, Byron's
valet – has already been related when telling Boatswain's story in Chapter I.

It is possible that Byron owned at least one other mastiff type during
these early Southwell days. Elizabeth Pigot, in the course of her humorous
poem about Byron and Boatswain, describes her mother and herself as being
so distraught at Byron's departure from Southwell with Boatswain that:

'They were near sinking under
And sharing the grave with his Lordship's dog, Thunder.'

Although we do not know how or when Thunder died, from his
name and other circumstantial evidence, it is a fair guess that he was
 another large dog of a mastiff type.

Many years later, Byron, in one of his melancholic humours, was to
complain that he could not even keep a dog alive which he liked, or which liked
him for any length of time. Although he probably had his favourite, Boatswain,
particularly in mind when expressing these thoughts, by the end of 1808 he
had already lost Thunder, Nelson, Savage (the bulldog pup) and Boatswain.

As to Boatswain's immediate successor, this was likely to have been
a mastiff. Byron himself confirms this in a gloomy letter to his half-sister,
Augusta, written from Newstead Abbey on 9th September 1811, having
just returned from his two-year tour of Greece and Albania: 'Since I lost
my Newfoundland dog I like nobody except his successor a Dutch mastiff.'
Byron's spirits were then at a particularly low ebb, as his mother and various
close friends of his adolescence – including the brilliant Charles Skinner
Matthews, tragically drowned in the Cam – had died in rapid succession.

We do not know the name of this mastiff. Byron referred to his dogs
more often than not by type, rather than by name. 'My mastiff', 'two new
mastiffs', 'the other mastiff' are typical examples. But although apparently

nameless, there is no doubt that this dog was to be Byron's prime, and possibly sole, canine companion during his four years of hectic fame, following the great success of the first two cantos of his 'Childe Harold' – a romantic pilgrimage in verse published in March 1812.

Byron said of himself, 'I awoke one morning and found myself famous'. For the next four years he was to be a literary star of London society, his patroness and confidante being the powerful Lady Melbourne, doyenne of Whig society. With his pale good looks, intriguing personality and amorous propensities he was involved in a succession of affairs with ladies of rank. If he was more pursued than the pursuer, the effect in the end was the same: he was the subject of speculation and gossip wherever he went.

Although burning the candle at both ends, he continued to produce a steady stream of highly successful romantic poems and even made a brief entry into politics in the Whig cause. At this time, he began to think seriously about marriage to a suitable heiress. His choice fell on Miss Anne Isabella Milbanke (Annabella) from Seaham in County Durham – a considerable heiress it is true, but a chaste bluestocking with an opinionated and improving turn of mind – whom he married on 2nd January 1815. It would be hard to conceive a more ill-suited couple as candidates for matrimony. On Byron's side, a certain admiration for her considerable intellectual qualities (she was good at mathematics – he called her the princess of parallelograms) and on hers, a desire to tame or improve, scarcely amounts to anything approaching a love match. And so it turned out. The marriage was a total disaster for the year it lasted.

Byron's financial affairs had become very difficult. On 10th December 1815, Annabella bore Byron a daughter baptised Augusta Ada. On 15th January 1816, she quit the debt-ridden conjugal mansion in Piccadilly – ostensibly to visit her parents at Kirkby Mallory in Leicestershire – but having secretly resolved never to live with Byron again.

It is not surprising that news of the mastiff or any other animals during this period when Byron's life was in turmoil, is scant. But the dog would almost certainly have been with him in London at his bachelor apartment in Albany, Piccadilly or at Newstead Abbey, where he returned occasionally to recuperate from the debilitating effects of his hectic social life. There is also good reason to believe that this mastiff accompanied Byron to the house he rented in Piccadilly during the year of his marriage. In an indirect way, the dog was to play some part in the final drama of Annabella's departure from Piccadilly and the collapse of his marriage. It is recounted by some biographers that, when passing the door of Byron's room (he had not troubled to rise to see her off) on the way down to the carriage with Ada early on the morning of 15th January, Annabella was tempted to throw herself down across the threshold on to the dog's mat and await all hazards; but it was only a moment and she passed on.

There is some confusion about the dog in question. One biographer refers to the mat as belonging to Boatswain's successor – a big Newfoundland dog. This is clearly incorrect, as Byron did not own another Newfoundland until 1823 (Lyon). Another biographer states that it was the mat on which Boatswain used to lie. We know Boatswain had died some eight years previously at Newstead and, although it is conceivable that Byron, for sentimental reasons, carried Boatswain's old mat around on his travels, there is a much more logical explanation: that this was the mat (perhaps Boatswain's at one time) on which Boatswain's immediate successor – the mastiff – used to lie outside his master's door while acting as night guard. He would have been part and parcel of that uneasy household, as Byron always liked to have at least one dog as companion and guard at all times. If the sight of that dog's mat had caused Annabella to pause a little longer for reflection on the course she was about to take, or even to have cast herself down upon it, then the chain of events which was to lead swiftly and irrevocably – despite Byron's initial surprise and opposition – to their legal separation, might never have begun. But it seems entirely in keeping with what is known of Annabella's character that the thought of so abject a surrender should have lasted 'but a moment'. Her actions were the very reverse of impulsive and her head was always firmly in command of her heart.

The gossip and scandal which erupted like a volcano in fashionable circles on the break-up of his marriage – including whispers of Byron's alleged sexual aberrations – threatened to engulf him. He was ostracised in society and deserted by fickle friends. Sick of the whole affair and its ugly aftermath, he resolved to quit England for good and did so on 25th April 1816.

It is not known what became of his mastiff, but bailiffs seized everything in his Piccadilly house shortly after he left, including some pets (a parrot and a squirrel). On his precipitate departure from England to the Continent, Byron took no dogs with him, but it was inevitable that before very long he would acquire some new canine companions. Mutz, the bobtailed Swiss drover's dog, was his first recorded purchase and Moretto the bulldog came later. It is also clear that Byron's dogs (and other pets) grew rapidly in number during his longish stay in Venice between 1817 and 1819 – particularly after he had rented the massive Palazzo Mocenigo on the Grand Canal. The sale of Newstead Abbey in 1817, to his old school friend Colonel Thomas Wildman for nearly £98,000 had transformed his financial position and allowed him to live in the grandiose style he had always wished for.

Byron's living quarters were on the first floor, while the ground floor just above canal level was virtually given over to his heavy baggage, the Napoleonic coach, carriages and a variety of pets – including a fox and two monkeys. In writing to John Cam Hobhouse on 6th April 1819, Byron adds a postscript which throws some light on his developing collection of pets; it mentions specifically the acquisition of 'two new mastiffs and Mutz is still in high old age'. The meaning of the word 'new' in this context is not completely clear, but the implication is that he already had others of this breed. This is more than likely, as mastiff types would have been the best all-purpose guard dogs for the great rambling Venetian palazzos. However, only a month later, on 21st May, he was writing to Hobhouse again and requesting, 'two bulldogs, a terrier and a Newfoundland'. A little later, he wrote to his publisher John Murray with a similar request, but on this occasion it was for one bulldog and two Newfoundlands. Doubtless all very confusing to those at the receiving end. It does show, however, that Byron's enthusiasm for dogs had not diminished.

We do not know the names of the two new mastiffs, but one at least moved with him and his household to Ravenna in 1819, where Byron had followed his latest and most enduring mistress – the young and delectable Countess Teresa Guiccioli. The Count, Teresa's husband, most obligingly (given the circumstances) let off part of his huge palazzo to Byron.

One of the mastiffs was almost certainly given away in the move to Ravenna. Byron gives specific instructions to his agent in Venice to have the 'other' mastiff sent, so one can only presume that he received the favoured one of the pair. This seems likely as, in a diary (the Ravenna Journal 4th Jan to 27th Feb 1821) which he kept for a short time while at Ravenna, an entry for January includes the following information: '....Played with my mastiff. Gave him his supper.' It was during this year in Ravenna that Byron demonstrated his generosity towards his fellow man, something which he did more often there than in London. When a man called Balani suffered a broken back rescuing Byron's dog from under a mill-wheel, Byron bestowed a pension on Balani's widow.

As mentioned already, the poet Shelley was astounded at the number and variety of Byron's pets, all wandering about at will in the Ravenna palazzo. He made a head count which included 'eight enormous dogs'. Of course, he may well have counted the same one several times over if they were all milling around, but even if he exaggerated a little, the number is still formidable. In an earlier letter to his half-sister Augusta, Byron mentions a total of six dogs, but the numbers would have waxed and waned quite rapidly through 'natural wastage' and other causes, the losses being made good haphazardly by further purchases as opportunity offered. From this total, the only dogs which can be positively identified are Mutz, Moretto and the favourite mastiff. There were probably other mastiff types among the balance as Shelley has described all the dogs he saw as 'enormous'.

In the summer of 1821, Teresa's family (her father was Count Gamba), who were Italian patriots and a thorn in the side of the Austrian ruling authorities, were exiled from Ravenna. Byron no longer had any reason to remain there and decided to move in September 1821 to Pisa to be near his friend Shelley, who had taken a house there. The move caused a tremendous upheaval in the Byron household and many of his pet animals, including some dogs, had to be disposed of or given away. In November, Byron occupied (with Teresa and her family) the Casa Lanfranchi at Pisa and, for the first time in Italy, gathered an English circle of friends and acquaintances about him. Among these was a person already referred to, Thomas Medwin, Shelley's cousin, an educated and well-travelled man who produced his book of 'Conversations with Byron' with unseemly speed after the poet's death in 1824. His book has been criticized by Byron scholars as inaccurate and fictitious in parts, but there is little reason to disbelieve his few remarks on Byron's dogs. These remarks provide a useful corroboration of circumstantial evidence to show that Byron probably only took two dogs with him from Ravenna to Pisa. According to Medwin, who arrived in Pisa about the time of the move, there were two dogs, a mastiff and a bulldog. The former would be the favourite mastiff first acquired in Venice, and the latter the bellicose Moretto.

Byron rented the Casa Lanfranchi on the river Arno, describing it as 'a famous old feudal palazzo'. Shelley and Mary Shelley were in a flat at the top of the Tre Palazzi di Chiesa, a house facing the Arno on the opposite bank from Byron's palazzo. The number of dogs at Pisa never built up to anything like the total at Ravenna and was probably a maximum of three. One other dog is known to have been added at Pisa. This was Medoro. He was a gift from a Captain Hay, one of Byron's circle of English friends in Ravenna, and it is known from the entry in Byron's steward Lega Zambelli's accounts for 24th March 1822 that Byron tipped the servant who brought the dog four crowns. As Doris Langley Moore has remarked, this was a large sum and perhaps more than it would have cost to buy the animal. Clearly, Medoro must have appealed greatly to Byron and, although there is no positive evidence to prove it, he also may have been of the mastiff family, given Byron's proclivity for large dogs. Lega Zambelli records in a later entry that a crown was spent on having the dogs' coats dipped (presumably against parasites). Byron certainly saw to it that his dogs received good food and proper care, even if their control was haphazard.

In 1822, the Gamba family were exiled yet again and took up residence in the Casa Saluzzo, Albaro, near Genoa. Byron joined them there, probably with the same three dogs he had at Pisa. As already mentioned Lyon, the young Newfoundland, was acquired here. Genoa was where Byron departed for Greece and we know that Lyon and Moretto accompanied Byron on the ill-fated expedition. It is likely that a third dog did so, too. This is borne out by John Cam Hobhouse's sighting of three of Byron's dogs playing on the deck of the Florida, the ship which brought Byron's body back to England. As to their disposal, Lyon went to Hobhouse and the other two to Henry Drury, Byron's tutor, at Harrow School.

*My tree*

***A Mastiff***
Oil on canvas
Richard Ansdell
1841

The Walker Art Gallery
National Museums Liverpool

One can deduce that either the favourite mastiff or Medoro (and he too may have been one) were at Missolonghi and survived Byron – that is unless he picked up a new dog in Greece, which is unlikely in the circumstances. The answer may never be known, but it has been shown that the mastiff type of dog was the most commonly owned of all the dogs in Byron's life. He certainly owned at least four, and probably several more, and these spanned every phase of his life.

*These two images illustrate the Regency love of the Newfoundland Landseer; both as a valued family member, and as a subject for narrative art. The gentle giants were, and are, noted for their remarkably placid temperament and life-saving abilities when anyone is in danger in the water.*

***Hats Off!***

***The family of N M Rothschild***

Oil on canvas

William Armfield Hobday

*c.* 1821

Reproduced with the permission of The Rothschild Archive
(Private Collection)

CHAPTER VI

# Lyon
# The Newfoundland

*Byron had now been in Italy for six years, living a peripatetic existence, moving from Palazzo to Palazzo as his whims or complicated affairs dictated, but despite this, managing to write perhaps his most important and controversial work – Don Juan.*

**Itchy feet**
Byron just couldn't sit still, despite his lameness. While in Italy he could have presented a TV travel show. Top row: Byron's balcony view of the Grand Canal from the Palazzo Mocenigo; his grand salon, and his gondolier's view of the day job. Below: the remains of Casa Gamba, Filetto, Ravenna; Pisa, and the Casa Saluzzo, Genoa.

**Visions of Byron**
© Nick Hugh McCann

As previously mentioned, in late 1822 Byron moved from Pisa to Albaro near Genoa where he shared the Casa Saluzzo with his mistress, Teresa Guiccioli, and some members of her family. Although now living quietly and in seeming contentment, he was in truth becoming heartily bored with the Italian scene. All his life he had hankered after a leading action role in some romantic cause and the opportunity was about to present itself. The Greeks were in a state of semi-open revolt against their Turkish masters and a London Committee of Philhellenes had been formed with the object of helping them throw off the Turkish yoke. Through his old friend John Cam Hobhouse, now a Whig M.P., Byron was approached and resolved to espouse the Greek cause actively, not only with monetary help, but by going there in person to act as a rallying point for Greek patriots and being prepared to fight if necessary.

His decision to set out for Greece was taken in May 1823 and at about this time, Edward Le Mesurier, a retired naval lieutenant and one of Byron's small circle of English friends and acquaintances, presented him with a young Newfoundland dog. Fifteen years had elapsed since the death of Boatswain and, although some of Byron's letters from Italy contained requests to his friends in England for the supply of a Newfoundland, none had been forthcoming. Byron was simply delighted and he promised Le Mesurier to take good care of him and 'never to part with him for any consideration'.

His name was Lyon or Lion. We cannot be certain of the exact spelling because Byron never committed his name to paper. Byron may have named him after his so-called wolf dog who had died many years previously and whose story is related in Chapter II. On the other hand, it is conceivable that by a coincidence Le Mesurier had already named him Lyon or Lion. From his picture posed with Byron at Missolonghi, he seems to have been a larger animal than Boatswain, and with his pendent ears and curly coat, more typical of the conventional Newfoundland of the day. He bears a striking similarity to Ben Marshall's Newfoundland painted in 1811.

Lyon's arrival seems to have been resented by Byron's other dogs (probably two at this time), namely the bellicose bulldog Moretto and Medoro (perhaps a mastiff type). On 11th May there is an entry in Lega Zambelli's account book recording the purchase of 'wine for washing the English dog'. It appears that cheap wine or vinegar was then used as a kind of antiseptic for wounds or bites and the presumption must be that Lyon had been involved in a scuffle or worse with the other dogs. Zambrelli had already purchased wine for the treatment of 'Medoro bitten by Moretto'.

Lyon and Moretto (and possibly Medoro) accompanied Byron on the fateful Greek adventure, which was to end so tragically with Byron's death at Missolonghi some nine months later. The expedition set out in July 1823 and progressed by way of the Island of Argostoli in Cephalonia – then under British rule – where Byron awaited developments and attempted to weigh up the relative effectiveness of the various political factions operating in the cause of Greek independence. Byron decided that Prince Mavrocordato was likely to prove the most reliable of the Greek leaders and sailed to join him at Missolonghi in western Greece.

The final passage, a relatively short one, which had to be made through Turkish-controlled waters, was not without considerable risk. Byron had hired two vessels for the voyage: a light, fast, sailing boat known as a Mistico and a larger, heavier boat called a Bombard. Byron embarked in the Mistico with most of his party, including Lyon, while Pietro Gamba (Teresa's brother) who had thrown in his lot with Byron, sailed with the horses, main baggage and stores in the Bombard. Moretto was in the Bombard party.

Before dawn on 31st December, Byron's party was startled by the sudden appearance of a Turkish frigate bearing down on it. It was indeed a delicate moment, but William Fletcher, Byron's faithful but ever-complaining valet (a Southwell man), recorded that – although the dogs had barked all night previously – they maintained a canny silence while in earshot of the Turkish warship. The Mistico managed to slip away from the Turkish ship and eventually, after several other adventures, reached her destination of Missolonghi on 5th January 1824. The slower Bombard was actually captured by a Turkish warship and might well have been sunk out of hand had it not turned out that the Master of the Bombard had once saved the Turkish captain's life when shipwrecked in the Black Sea. The Bombard was escorted into Patras but after much polite palaver, including the handing over of 'gifts', was finally released and made her way successfully to Missolonghi.

Much has been written of Byron's four months at Missolonghi and of his Herculean endeavours, against all the odds, to maintain cohesion, discipline and a sense of purpose among a motley band of 'Suliotes' – irregulars from various provinces to whom money spoke louder than patriotism – as well as some foreign 'experts' who were supposed to provide technical expertise. He had also to contend with the well-intentioned inanities of the London Committee who placed printing presses and tracts before the necessities of war.

Initially, hopes had been high that Byron's force might be able to wrest Lepanto from the Turks, but that prospect gradually faded through procrastination, disaffection and intrigue. The complex problems with which Byron was faced, coupled with the appalling weather, rapidly undermined his health, although not his resolve. In this trying period Lyon was to prove Byron's devoted and faithful companion, and one with whom he could seek escape and relaxation in playful banter from the problems around him.

Byron and his immediate entourage occupied a large, damp house in Missolonghi, surrounded by a number of outbuildings. His personal bodyguard, consisting of Suliotes, armed to the teeth, were housed in one of these large outer rooms. William Parry, the fire-master sent out by the London Committee to organise a small artillery force and to supervise the defences of Missolonghi, whose practical common sense Byron came to value greatly, had recorded graphically the great mutual affection between dog and master. Byron had been greatly affected by what he regarded as the personal betrayal of some of his Suliotes who left with some of his monies to join the opposing side in what was tantamount to a civil war in Greece at this time. As we have read in Chapter I, on the inscription on Boatswain's memorial plinth, Byron saw his dog as ever faithful but man as having vices.

**Opposite:**
*Dog-day afternoon*

An engraving by Robert Seymor from a sketch by Parry of Milord and Lyon, from *The Last Days of Lord Byron,* by William Parry

Private Collection

**In the dog house**

A recreation of Parry
sketching Byron with
Lyon in the bleak and
squalid surroundings
of Headquarters
Missolonghi.

*Visions of Byron*
© Nick Hugh McCann

Byron, especially on wet days, was wont to visit his Suliote guard in their quarters and according to Parry: 'On such occasions he was almost always accompanied by his favourite dog Lyon who was perhaps his dearest and most affectionate friend. They were indeed very seldom separated. Riding or walking, sitting or standing, Lyon was his constant attendant. He can scarcely be said to have forsaken him even in his sleep. Every evening did he go to see that his master was safe before he lay down himself and then he took up his station close to the door, a guard certainly as faithful, though not so efficient, as Lord Byron's corps of Suliotes.'

After Byron's death, Parry wrote a book in 1825 entitled 'The Last Days of Lord Byron' in which he tells us of Byron and his relationship with Lyon: 'With Lyon Lord Byron was accustomed, not only to associate, but to commune very much, and very often. His most usual phrase was, "Lyon you are no rogue, Lyon". The dog's eyes sparkled and his tail swept the floor as he sat with his haunches on the ground. "Thou art more faithful than men, Lyon; I trust thee more". Lyon sprang up and bounded round his master as much as to say, "You may trust me, I will watch actively on every side." "Lyon I love thee, thou art my faithful dog!" And Lyon jumped and kissed his master's hand, as an acknowledgement of his homage. In this sort of mingled talk and gambol Lord Byron passed a good deal of time, and seemed more contented, more calmly self-satisfied, on such occasions, than almost on any other. In conversation and in company he was animated and brilliant; but with Lyon and in stillness he was pleased and perfectly happy.'

Parry was a tough old campaigner not normally given to mawkish sentimentality, hence the above description deserves to be treated with respect. It also shows Byron expounding again his old theme of a dog's simple faithfulness and man's duplicity – and perhaps the words were never more truly uttered than at Missolonghi where many sought to take advantage of him. There is an earlier amusing tale involving Lyon recorded by James Forrester of the English gun-brig 'Alacrity', when he came ashore with his Captain to confer with Byron about an incident to a neutral vessel. After a good dinner at which Byron was in high spirits, he asked if the principal guest would care to indulge in some pistol practice against bottles set up at 15 paces. The challenge was accepted and Byron demonstrated his usual skill at this sport, which amazed Forrester. Furthermore, after every shot, Lyon would rush to retrieve the remains of the bottle and lay it at his master's feet much to the amusement of those watching.

On 9th April 1824 Byron developed a severe fever, having been caught out riding in a heavy rainstorm and remaining soaked through for several hours. His health had been declining markedly since February and this proved to be the final blow. The remedies prescribed by the two young doctors who attended him were disastrous – the then universal panacea of bleeding the patient was rigorously applied, but desanguination only further weakened Byron, who died on 19th April. Amidst the great grief of those around him and the whole Greek nation, his body was embalmed and returned to England (with his effects and some members of his party) on the barque Florida.

It is known for certain that Lyon accompanied his master's body home on the Florida. John Cam Hobhouse managed to board the vessel at Gravesend as she made her way up river. As he neared her, sad memories were awakened by the sight of three dogs playing on the deck. One of these was Lyon, who was subsequently given to Hobhouse by Augusta Leigh, Byron's half-sister. Hobhouse must have appreciated the gift of this sagacious and lovable great dog, knowing him to have been his friend's devoted companion in the last few tragic months of his life. But much to the anguish and chagrin of Hobhouse, Lyon died in 1825 from some unknown cause only a year after his arrival in England.

The circumstances surrounding Lyon's death were to lead to a row between Hobhouse and the vet who attended the dog. This was none other than William Youatt whose book Hobhouse was later to sponsor and whose views on matters canine are quoted extensively here. Youatt had come to hear that Hobhouse had 'blown his top' on the death of Lyon and that he had called him 'a fool, an ass and a dolt'. Youatt sought to defend himself against these allegations in the following letter to Hobhouse: ' ...the associated names of Byron and Hobhouse rendered the animal most interesting to me – my best and warmest feelings were identified with the recovery of that dog. You, Sir, know that it was a complicated case. You know the disadvantages under which every vet labours whose patients can tell neither the nature nor the seat of the pain. I knew he was not well. I dreamed not of so speedy a death. This an ignorant man might say proves me to be a fool, ass, the dolt which you describe. From you I expected a more liberal and juster decision'.

Youatt's florid literary style is unmistakable but his plaint has a becoming ring of humility which apparently placated Hobhouse sufficiently for him to deny that he had ever spoken insultingly and to enclose a donation to a charitable cause for animals. The vet responded with an acknowledgement of his 'unfeigned pleasure' and an admission of his misgivings after dispatching his remonstrance.

Hobhouse apparently saw no reason to commemorate Lyon with all the paraphernalia of monuments and inscriptions which Byron had lavished on Boatswain. Instead he found an appropriately pleasant spot in which to lay the dog to rest. Lyon's grave was under the willow tree near the water at Whitton, Hounslow, Hobhouse's country seat.

### *Moon River*

As soon as Byron's remains arrived back
in England, the rumours and scandal
were re-ignited.

After the body was taken from the ship,
*The Florida*, it lay in state in Sir Edward
Knatchbull's house in Great George St,
Westminster. Despite repeated requests,
he was not allowed a burial in Westminster
Abbey's *Poet's Corner*.

His memoirs were burnt by ill-judged well-
wishers, careful of their own reputations by
association, thereby carrying out one of the
greatest pieces of desecretion of literature
in the English language.

The funeral procession, through London to
Highgate Hill and to the north, was witnessed
by tens of thousands of people. Some carriages
of the aristocracy were present but empty –
representing quiet but meaningful snubs. They
had not forgotten the scandals of 1816.

When the procession reached Kentish Town,
Mary Shelley, the author of *Frankenstein*, who
had known Byron well, saw it go by, as did
Caroline Lamb, when it passed Brocket Hall in
Hertfordshire on its way to Nottinghamshire.

Aged only 36, akin to all superstars who die
young, Byron became a legend.

**Lord Byron's Lyon**
Oil on canvas
Nick Hugh McCann

Private Collection

© Nick Hugh McCann

CHAPTER VII

# Dogs Miscellaneous

*Poodle Parlour*

*Trial by Jury, or Laying Down the Law c.* **1840**

Oil on canvas
Sir Edwin Landseer (1802 – 1873)

*The previous chapters have dealt with the main breeds of dogs which Byron owned: Newfoundlands, mastiffs, bulldogs together with Lyon the wolf-dog and Mutz, or Short Tail, the Swiss drover's dog. There were other dogs in Byron's life which are revealed briefly in his correspondence or from other sources and to complete the story of Byron's dogs, what is known of them is as follows.*

# FANNY - A TERRIER

Although Byron had a particular liking for large, even massive dogs, when living at Southwell, Nottinghamshire, in his boyhood he owned a small terrier bitch called Fanny. Fanny was contemporary with Nelson and Boatswain and appears to be not only the smallest of Byron's numerous dogs but also the only bitch (which can be positively identified as such). Byron was very fond of her, and on several occasions asked after Fanny's health when writing to Elizabeth Pigot, his confidante and fellow dog lover at Southwell. One such extract from a letter written from Trinity College, Cambridge in 1807, reads as follows: 'Talking of women puts me in mind of my terrier Fanny – how is she?'

As dogs were not allowed in college rooms at Cambridge, Fanny and the rest of the dogs had to remain under the care of servants at Burgage Manor, Southwell during term time, under supervision by Mrs Byron. Elizabeth Pigot who lived across Burgage Green from the Manor, also kept a watchful eye on Byron's dogs who were given to roaming around Southwell. The Pigots' house was visited frequently by Byron when he was at home and wished to escape from his temperamental mother.

Although Mrs Byron's own terrier, the feisty Gilpin, was for a long time Boatswain's tormentor, relations between Fanny and Boatswain seem to have been most amiable. This is borne out by a verse in Elizabeth's poem about Byron and Boatswain, which mentions Boatswain and Fanny playing together:

'He [Byron] went to the Club to eat oysters with many,
And on his return found him (Boatswain), playing with Fanny.'

If Fanny possessed the main characteristics of the early 19th century English terrier as described by William Youatt, she would have been smallish and of wiry build with a short coat (rough or smooth), a pointed muzzle, prominent eyes, ears half erect, probably black in colour with a yellowish spot over the eyes. The variations in these characteristics would have been very considerable even 200 years ago, and today the generic terrier type is split up into numerous well-defined and recognised breeds. Youatt describes the uses of the terrier as being mainly in the destruction of vermin around the farm or estate, and also with fox hounds for getting a fox out of its earth when it has gone to ground.

Fanny faded from the picture when Byron left Southwell in September 1808 and occupied Newstead Abbey for a short time before setting out on his tour of Greece and Albania in 1809. Mrs Byron moved to Newstead Abbey for the two years that Byron was away and attempted to look after his interests. Fanny may have been with her, although she may have been boarded out to tenant farmers or given away. It is not known if she lived until Byron's return.

Much later when in Italy, Byron wrote to his friend Hobhouse, and also to his publisher John Murray, requesting the dispatch of a terrier from England. For what purpose would he have needed one? Almost certainly for the control of rats, which would have been legion in the damp rambling palazzos. Youatt claimed that a terrier was in his very element as a rat killer and cites the exploits of the legendary 19th-century ratting terrier, Billy: 100 rats killed in just over six minutes! As in the case of his request for bulldogs and Newfoundlands to be sent from England, this one does not seem to have been met; but as his friends were hard put to keep him supplied with the toilet essentials and the books he liked, perhaps this is not too surprising.

*A Master at Work*

*Three Dogs*
Sir Edwin Landseer (1802-1873)
Coloured chalks on blue paper
June 24th, 1803

### Top Hat & Tail

Commissioned by Queen Victoria and presented to Prince Albert at Christmas 1841. Prince Albert's favourite greyhound bitch, Eos, stands poised and alert, guarding her master's possessions – his leather gloves, top hat and ivory-topped cane. A deerskin footstool with hoof feet symbolises the Prince's sporting interests.

### Eos

Oil on canvas
Sir Edwin Landseer
(1803 – 1873), 1841

© HM The Queen

# GREYHOUNDS

The greyhound is one of the earliest recorded dogs and is depicted in ancient Egyptian tomb art. The poet Ovid describes the coursing of the hare:

'As when th' impatient greyhound, slipped from far,
bounds o'er the glade to course the fearful hare.'

There are references to greyhounds in two of Byron's letters. The first of these, written while at Newstead Abbey shortly after Boatswain's death was addressed to 'Gentleman' John Jackson, the renowned prize-fighter, who had instructed Byron in the noble art of self defence while at Cambridge. Byron had struck up a firm friendship with Jackson, to whom he looked for advice on sporting matters generally. The relevant extract reads as follows: '...You will get the greyhound from the owner at any price and as many more of the same breed (male or female) as you can collect... I am sorry you should have so much trouble. I was not aware of the difficulty of procuring the animal in question...'

This is certainly a strongly worded request – virtually a command – and with a note of desperation about it. One wonders whether it was brought about by the tragic death of Boatswain less than a month before. He may have felt that a greyhound, with its grace and beauty of form, could fill the void in his affections. Unfortunately, we do not know the outcome of this request, but in any case a few months later Byron sailed for Europe and was gone for two years, so he would not have been able to enjoy his new purchase for long.

Byron wrote in September 1813 to his friend James Wedderburn Webster who lived in Rotherham: 'My love to the faithless Nettle, (who I daresay is wronging me during my absence.' Nettle was a poodle which Webster had given to Byron.

However, it would appear that greyhounds were still on his mind during his journey through Greece and he managed to obtain one there which in a letter home, he tersely records as having died on the passage to England. This greyhound may have been of the Grecian variety, which Youatt states to be similar to the English breed except that, 'it is not so large, the muzzle is not so pointed and the limbs are not so finely framed'. In other words, a kind of roughish country cousin of our own native breed. It is indeed a pity that Byron failed to get him home and no reason is given for his death.

It is entirely in keeping with Byron's character that he should have wished to own greyhounds – surely the swiftest and most graceful of all our sporting dogs, with a noble lineage of great antiquity. But regrettably he does not appear to have met with much success in that direction.

THE GREYHOUND.

A NOBLE POET — Scratching up his Ideas.

# Bibliography

In the first chapter I mention a book published in 1852 which went to many editions – namely 'The Dog' by William Youatt. Without his knowledgeable work on 19th-century breeds of dogs I would have found difficulty in writing much of this book. I now recite the principal printed works I have consulted in writing this book and list them:-

BEATON, Roderick, 'Byron's War', Cambridge University Press 2013

BOND, G C, 'Lord Byron and the Newfoundland', Newfoundland Club Newsletter, Winter 2001

BROWN Iain G, 'Abbbotsford & Sir Walter Scott', Ed Society of Antiquaries, Scotland 2003

GROSSMAN, Loyd, 'The Dog's Tale' BBC Books 1993

JESSIE, Edward, 'Anecdotes of Dogs', Bell & Daldy, London 1873

KENYON-JONES, Christine, 'Kindred Brutes – Animals in Romantic-Period Writing', Ashgate 2001

MARCHAND, Leslie A, 'Byron: A Biography', Alfred A Knopf, New York 1957

MARCHAND, Leslie A, 'Byron's Letters & Journals', John Murray London 1976-1994

MOORE, Doris Langley, 'Lord Byron Accounts Rendered', John Murray London 1974

PENDRED, Gerald, 'Lord Byron and his Dogs', article Pedigree Digest, Vol 14 June 1988

SMITH, Christine, 'Lord Byron A Dog's Best Friend', article Kennel Gazette, August 1991

WATERS, Nick, 'The Newfoundland Heritage & Art', BB Press, Netherlands 2006

YOUATT, William, 'The Dog', Longman, London 1852

# Epilogue

*Byron has brought me so many friends from around the world and huge dividends from the study of this amazing man and his times.*

**Byron society**

**Geoffrey Bond with Landseer Newfoundland, Cruz and right, black Newfoundland, Damian.**

**In the distance is the West Front of Newstead Abbey, and to the left one of the Wicked Lord's 17th century forts, now a residential property.**

**Photograph by Nigel Gibson of *Weave Creative*, Nottingham**

© Nigel Gibson

Many books have been written about Byron, seeking to interpret and understand his life and work. He has been a rich source of study in the English departments of universities around the world. Biographers have at times mentioned his love of animals – this book I believe is the first devoted entirely to Byron and his love of dogs.

I have an extensive Byron library and have read much about the poet as well as a great deal of his poetry. However, my studies of his relationships with animals, dogs in particular, have given me a greater insight into his personality and increased my understanding of the man. Byron had a difficult, fatherless childhood with a mother who used sometimes to refer to him as 'a lame brat'. He was unexpectedly pitched into the aristocracy, but remained an outsider. His dogs gave him affection and obedience, love of a canine kind, unquestioning and without demand.

In terms of modern care, dogs are used to comfort the sick and the elderly – they are one of the few animal species who will be devoted to a Master, even without any great reward. I have, in this book of Byron and 'his friends', demonstrated what an integral and important part they played in his life. I see Byron as a colossus of his times, striding through the literary landscape – always with a dog, or dogs, at his side.

**Geoffrey Bond**

### *The Pilgrim of Eternity*

...reclines in rapture on a divan of Gordon tartan, as the goddess of poetry sprinkles him with the dust of inspiration. Within the scheme are people and places he remembers well: Mary Chaworth; Teresa Guiciolli; Burgage Manor; Cape Sunium; the Winged Lion of Venice; Lake Geneva; Chateau Chillon; The Acropolis in Athens; Pena Palace in Cintra, Portugal and the Falls of Terni in Italy. On the bedside table is the famous skull cup. Beside the angel is a Newfoundland dog and Byron's homeric helmet.

### *Byron's Dream* (mural), commissioned by the author
*Liquitex* acrylic on plaster with a trompe l'oeil painted frame, 10ft x 6ft
Nick Hugh McCann 1992

©Nick Hugh McCann
Private Collection

# Acknowledgements

The author would like to thank:
Charlotte Bond for marketing advice
Carol Bruce his Secretary for typing manuscripts
Dr Iain Gordon Brown
Brian Butler my Library Advisor
Byron Societies of the world
Professor Richard Cardwell
Dr Peter Cochran and Dr Christine Kenyon-Jones for scholarly advice
Linda Croose-Smith & Nigel Gibson for photography
Sarah Davison for editorial assistance & proof reading
Elaine Dickson for the loan of her Newfoundland Damian
Loyd Grossman for his Foreword
The Kennel Club
Brenda King of the Newfoundland Club
John Murray Publishers for kind permission to reproduce Byron paintings
Nottingham City Corporation for kind permission to reproduce paintings,
photographs and for location access
The Rothschild Archive for permission to reproduce their painting
Sonia Solicari & The Guildhall Art Gallery, City of London Corporation
Rick Watson, Head of Reference Services Harry Ransom Center,
University of Texas at Austin, USA
Ally & Sue Walden for loan of their Newfoundland Cruz
Jack Wasserman, New York
Where appropriate within the text acknowledgement and permission to
reprint pictures and drawings has been made

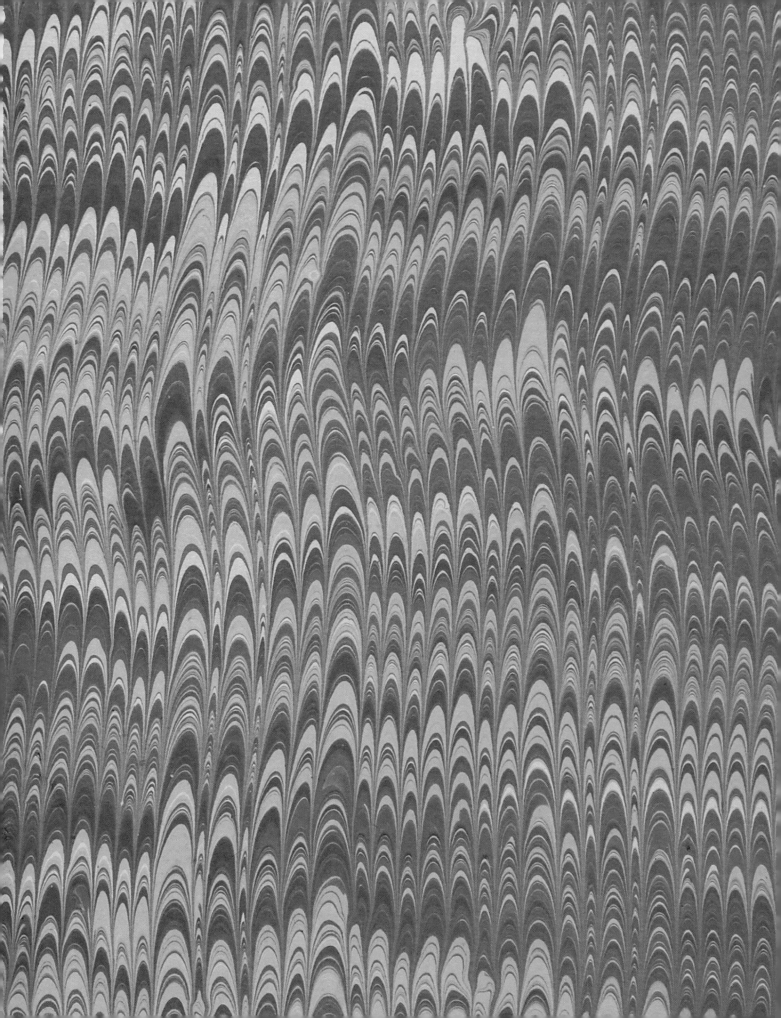